Reforming the Prophet

also by W.R. Clement

Quantum Jump

Reforming the Prophet

THE QUEST FOR THE ISLAMIC REFORMATION

W.R. CLEMENT

INSOMNIAC PRESS

Edited and designed by Richard Almonte
Copy edited by Jan Barbieri

National Library of Canada Cataloguing in Publication Data
Clement, W. R. (Wilfrid Reid)

Reforming the prophet : the quest for the Islamic reformation / W.R. Clement.

Includes bibliographical references and index.
ISBN 1-894663-29-2

1. Islamic renewal. 2. Islamic fundamentalism. 3. Islam and politics.
4. Islam—21st century. I. Title.

BP60.C46 2002   297'.09'051   C2002-903818-9

The publisher gratefully acknowledges the support of the Canada Council, the Ontario Arts Council and the Department of Canadian Heritage through the Book Publishing Industry Development Program.

Printed and bound in Canada

Insomniac Press, 192 Spadina Avenue, Suite 403,
Toronto, Ontario, Canada, M5T 2C2
www.insomniacpress.com

This book is dedicated to Master Jackson Thomas Norman Matthews and Ms. Lily Riley Boyd-Bell in the hope that they will enjoy long lives and that this book will prove to be completely wrong.

CONTENTS

Introduction

AT THIS PERIOD in history when many North Americans are discovering Islam and its variations for the first time, we are frequently told that the Muslim world is about to undergo a reformation that may or may not be every bit as significant to world history as was the Protestant Reformation in sixteenth-century Europe.

That such a reformation may not be immediately welcomed by the greater Muslim population, and, if successful, may not be without searing cost to the people of the Islamic world, is something that proponents of a reformation have not seen as a significant outcome. But of course, any attempt at reformation in Islam will necessarily be global in reach. Unlike the Protestant Reformation, which rode on the coattails of the humanistic Renaissance, the Islamic reformation has its intellectual underpinnings in the Islamic legal system (Shari'a). This reformation will attempt to avoid a Westernization of the Islamic legal code which could occur under the influence of the twin forces of international commercial harmonization and the human rights heavys from both the United Nations and the newly activist International Court of Justice at the Hague. After all, who knows when the court will expand its mandate from war crimes cases and move on to aping its betters by trying human rights cases like the European Union Court in Strassbourg?

Islam has no centralized authority from which it draws any sort of localized guidance. The closest the Muslim world comes to a central authority is the self-selecting group of clerics known as the Ulama. The Ulama can only voice opinions, and even this usually long after the event raising the question at issue has transpired. In Islam, a ruling of faith has the force of law because Islam is a religious coating to a legal system with no central authority. Such a ruling can come from an imam (a leader of a mosque) and can be, if not completely binding, at least taken seriously by all Muslins worldwide.

A few simple facts: Islam commands 1.1 billion followers. It is primarily concentrated from the Atlantic coast of North Africa to Central Asia and down to Indonesia, which is the world's most populous Islamic country. India has the world's second largest Muslim population. The world's most common name is Mohammed. There are more followers of Islam living in the United States and Canada than there are adherents of Judaism.

It is of compelling interest for non-Islamic countries to avoid becoming involved in the forthcoming attempts at an Islamic Reformation and to resist meddling in what is essentially a Muslim family quarrel. Islam is so culturally incompatible with Western cultural values that it would be a major public relations job to encourage the Western world to take an interest in Muslim events. After all, the Islamic world has wisely avoided being drawn into the West's reformations, on the grounds that the arguments were too weird to understand.

This admonition of Western values holds in spite of the claims for potential profit from European and North American commercial interests. It holds against allegations of humanitarian imperatives or the opportunity for territorial gain. It hold against the chances for military glory and the resulting domestic political benefits available to those who claim that production of transient victories during times of domestic political unrest is good for the tranquility and continuity of domestic governance.

Reformations are unpleasant and messy affairs. Our own Western reformation has scarred our history from the fifteenth century to the present day, as can be attested to by anyone who has watched various well-wishing, or merely self-interested, parties trying to broker peace deals in Northern Ireland, East Timor, India and Pakistan, or Palestine and Israel.

There is no doubt that the imminent reformation in the Islamic world will affect the rest of the globe in nasty ways. We must however resist becoming an agent of global religious power-broking whenever possible. One thing to keep in mind, for instance, is that the supporters of an Islamic reformation are a miniscule minority in the Muslim world. This minority is supported by a host of Western media advocates, whose view is that if Muslims would only get out of the seventh century and become like the rest of us, the world could get on with its business of becoming a globalized economy made in the image and likeness of the West.

The impetus for this book came in the wake of 9/11 when many leading pundits were suggesting that the Islamic world simply had to undergo a reformation. They argued that this was the only solution to the problem of Islamic fundamentalists who were targeting the West for its championship in the evolutionary development of state-ordered legalisms. In response, the fundamentalists claimed the West espoused a legal system totally unrelated to Qur'anic or other religious regulation, by its promulgation of the secular state as the basis for the post-World War II economy. The West's support for Israel is seen by the fundamentalists as a vehicle for its refusal to accommodate or to even recognize the legitimacy of Islamic *Shari'a* law.

Since World War II Islamic communities have been concerned with recovering a theocratic state with the Islamic legal system. Essentially, this theocratic state is a legal system in the garb of a religion, set in place by Mohammed more than a thousand years ago. Because the legal system is an integral part of the religion, the laws are revelations from Allah, which means a law-abiding person is de facto a faith-adhering person.

In the middle of the eighteenth century there arose a puritanical Muslim sect, the Wahhabi, which came in time to sponsor the rise of a new Arabian dynasty, the House of Sa'ud. The Wahhabis led a fundamentalist movement that established and armed the Arab armies that led the overthrow of the Ottoman Empire following World War I in 1918. This defeat of the Ottoman Sultan created a power vacuum after 1918 that allowed for the expansion of Wahhabi doctrine under the political leadership of King Ibn Sa'ud of Saudi Arabia. Ibn Sa'ud quickly moved to occupy Mecca and Medina, the holiest cities of Islam. He placed these sites under the religious control of the Wahhabis and placed the pilgrim-age revenues firmly in his own control. While the post-World War II world saw the emergence of a number of "Islamic" states, it was the cultural and economic power of the United States that got the attention of the Madrasses (Islamic religious schools) and teachers who ran them.

These Madrasses have attracted financial support from Muslims who made significant fortunes in the Islamic world in retailing (after graduating from the bazaar economy of the souks), resource recovery (large-ly oil), construction and various other investments of the type that are available to those with large capital pools and excellent investment managers (i.e., banks in Switzerland, London and New York).

Islam was established as a religion that would order a world of nomadic people into an extended family, patri-arch-centred domestic environment. Muslims adhere to a faith that has never been really big on centralization. The Madrasses out in the provinces, for instance, don't as a rule pay a whole lot of attention to the Oxford/Harvard equivalent in the Muslim world. The Islamic al-Azhar University is the home base of the Ulama and is located in a vintage section of Cairo. It is an interesting place. If you ever wanted to see what a scholastic university in feudal/manorial Europe looked like, al-Azhar is the place to go. Similarly, if you want to get a glimpse of a mosque from the past days of Muslim glory, look up the Sultan al-Ghari Mosque located about a block away from al-Azhar University. With its beauti-ful carpets and ornamentation, the al-Ghari mosque is a major example of Islamic architecture of 500 years ago. It is the here that the Ulama of al-Azhar University go to worship.

While researching this book I was constantly reminded of Paul Kennedy's book *The Rise and Fall of the Great Powers*. Here Kennedy, a Yale economic historian, sets out to study economic change and military conflict from 1500 to 2000. This genuinely distinguished American historian shocked economists, historians and political analysts with his findings.

When *Rise and Fall* was published, it was eagerly greeted by a host of scholars who fell on the great man's words only to find that Kennedy had posited a very controversial theory. He argued that the collapse of empires, great powers and superpowers came down to the proposition that eventually the great powers will go broke trying to maintain their legions on the far-flung borders of their empire. This bankruptcy can occur from fighting external invaders or from having to cool out national rebellions. Kennedy's theory was, of course, meticulously and massively documented.

Kennedy's peers tried to poke holes in the black hole he had painted, but the result was the opposite: Kennedy's thesis has become the consensus in the intervening years since it was published in 1988. The disturbing thought is which civilization, the West or Islam, is the one in decline.

This book is divided into two sections. The first is a brief look back at our own Western reformation. It is a reminder of our own brush with a religious reform movement that will serve as a benchmark to concisely explore what reformations are all about and the extent to which they influence us. The second section is a look at some of the problems Muslims will face if they are going to have a big reform event themselves. I will suggest that the truth is that Islam's structure is so circumscribed that the Muslim world has no choice except to disintegrate. The Islamic fundamentalists argue the Islamic states permit them to maintain their religion without interference. Yet theocracies are very difficult to maintain in the pluralistic secular world we have crafted for ourselves. Islam has to have a reformation, but reformations require big changes, something everyone finds very uncomfortable and divisive.

Many in the West currently see themselves as hostages held by sentient beings whose arguments defy their own sense of history. As we progress along the events of the information age firm in the knowledge that this is the main road to a shining future, adherents of Islam pop up on our horizon from nowhere with a vision of medieval feudal glory.

Sentience is a questionable commodity in any reformation. All of the world's major religions, except Islam, have gone through reformations. Even a cursory glance at the history of world-class reformations makes it plain that no one aspiring to or claiming to be a sentient being, would wish to participate in a reformation. The problem is that the world is quickly shrinking, metaphorically at least, and the spillover of Islam's adventure in reforming itself is bound to be global in its repercussions.

WRC

Toronto, June 2002

Chapter One

Strange New Guys in Town:
Early Adopters of the Reformation

BEFORE WE EXPLORE the possibility and the probability of an Islamic Reformation, it might be a useful exercise to revisit our own past and look at the European Protestant Reformation and its precursors. If nothing else, such a reference to our own past will give us some idea of the generic problems in setting out to reform a major world religion. After all, we hear the voices of our own political pundits calling for such a reform movement and we often have no idea about what is in store for us and for the billion-plus Muslims who will have to deal with the discomforts that reformations cause. Furthermore, we will get an opportunity to examine the breadth of human responses that come out when you put a reformation on offer.

The European Protestant Reformation of Luther, Calvin and Henry VIII of England had many precursors. It didn't just happen out of the blue. Anyone with an intact central nervous system and a keen mind with the 20/20 vision that comes from being mentally based in the twenty-first centur, knows that people such as the Cathars, the Hussites and John Wycliffe, as well as countless other, less well-known actors in the church reform movement across Europe, caused the Reformation as much as the well-known historical figures mentioned earlier.

In 1208, while the Crusaders were putting the Frankish kingdom of Jerusalem at risk from the Muslim forces, Pope Innocent III found he had to turn his attention to another, more potent enemy, the Cathars. Pure and simple, the Cathars were a heresy powered by particularly effective preachers. This new enemy was a threat to the Church's posture of universality. It was a serious move for the papacy to drop the Crusaders to take up war with the Cathars, but then again, the Cathars were serious people.

Sometimes called Albigenses, after a town in Northern Italy, the Cathars challenged the Church on matters of doctrine that wouldn't raise any kind of interest today. They rekindled the third-century heresies of Manichaenism and Gnosticism from the church in Alexandria along with a clear commitment to reincarnation. All of this, combined with the Cathars' popular appeal, was a no-no and had been banned at the Council of Nicea in 325 AD.

Pope Innocent quickly put together an army and set off to put a stop to this heretical movement. This was only one of the precursors to the Reformation.

Vernacular Bibles Become Best-sellers

John Wycliffe (c. 1330–1384) was popular philosophy professor at Oxford at at time when being a popular professor was like being a contemporary rock star. In 1360 Wycliffe became the master of Balliol College. He then resigned the mastership to take a college living. As a master, Wycliffe was not required to teach regular classes. Being granted a college living meant that Wycliffe would be supported by the college while not having to do administrative work.

Eventually Wycliffe became the parish priest of Lutterworth in Leicestershire. Somehow he became the leader of a dissident band of followers known as Lollards that included some of the aristocracy and assorted gentry. His real role was as a propagandist and spokesman for the theological concerns that were intermingled with the political concerns of the day.

One of Wycliffe's coterie was John of Gaunt, who was the duke of Lancaster and son of King Edward III. Among the other followers listening to John Wycliffe were a large number of parish clergy and academic theologians from Oxford. Wycliffe also held a consultant's job at the court in London where he wrote pamphlets and fulfilled various propaganda jobs.

In 1374 he was sent by the leaders of the Lollards to Bruges, in what is now Belguim, to meet with papal representatives. At issue were Wycliffe's and his followers' claims of various ecclesiastical abuses. The pope's lawyers found that what Wycliffe was claiming as abuses were at variance with their own views of these events. Wycliffe was prosecuted.

At his trial Wycliffe raised his views against the Church hierarchy and the powers given to priests. That these views were somewhat negative is an understatement. He passed out pamphlets and tracts written not in Latin, but in English, which expressed his views on transubstantiation. Wycliffe held that the bread and wine given at communion were not miraculously converted to the "body and blood of Christ." His attitude failed again to pass the test of acceptability of the papal lawyers' views on Church doctrine.

Wycliffe also chose this moment in history to issue the first translation of the Bible in English, which was seen as a blow to the Church's claims of universalit. The pope's dream team of legal hounds pretty well knew what they had on their hands. Surprisingly Wycliffe was not condemned; unsurprisingly, his ideas were vilified in the strongest terms, but he was still allowed to return to Lutterworth.

He soon became involved in another controversy about Church doctrinal and constitutional issues. Wycliffe held that secular authorities had control over the clergy in civil disputes, which set the English bishops' teeth grinding. In 1376 he came out with a little paper called *De Domino,* which suggested that rulers get their power by grace alone and therefore, all evil, bad or wicked rulers are unfit to rule. This assertion is like the Puritan belief that salvation comes from faith alone and that anyone without faith will not enjoy salvation.

De Domino got Wycliffe called before the Archbishop of England at the Lambeth Palace office. The summons failed to have the desired effect, however, as a nasty brawl broke out between the bishop of London and Wycliffe's friend, follower and patron, John of Gaunt. This brawl was so distasteful to the archbishop that he closed down the proceedings.

On hearing of these procedural problems, Pope Gregory XI first banned Wycliffe, then wrote bulls to Oxford, to the bishops and to the king, demanding they arrest Wycliffe and bring him before the archbishop. After the Bruges fiasco this could only turn out badly. Wycliffe had tested the Church's constitutional edifice, questioned the priestly power of absolution, called for an end to enforced confession, questioned the efficacy of penances and indulgences and, finally, called for the right to read the Bible in the vernacular, yet little was done to Wycliffe. Having patrons like John of Gaunt and followers that included half of the magnates in England had certain benefits.

Wycliffe next founded an order of preachers called "poor priests" who spoke to the people in English and read the Bible to them in English. Wycliffe went back to Lutterworth where he spent the remainder of his life writing more pamphlets in English and finishing his Bible translation. After his death in 1384, his ideas enjoyed a period of wide influence. Yet his followers, the Lollards, were victims of mass arrests and forced recantation. Jan Hus was reported to be a follower of Wycliffe and, at the very least, was deeply influenced by him.

New Heresies Pressure the Church's Investigative Resources

Another precursor event to the Reformation was promoted by Jan Hus (*c.* 1372–1415) from Bohemia, who was a professor and later Dean of Philosophy at Charles University in Prague. Hus spoke of the inequities involved in the Church owning half the land in the Kingdom of Bohemia. He also spoke out against the trade in indulgences, as Luther would do more successfully in about a hundred years and as Wycliffe had already done in England. Hus collected the usual suspects around his do-it-yourself heresy and enjoyed wide popular support. After the usual massacres, Hus was burned at the stake upon being found a heretic by the Council of Constance in 1415.

Composers Get Cool Licks in Switch to Pops and Polyphony

An unlikely source of pre-Reformation challenge to the established order came from the world of music. This was the genre of so-called Franco-Flemish music, or Renaissance polyphony, which had its beginning around 1420. A new view of causality in the late medieval and early Renaissance periods made enigmas long believed to be inaccessible approachable through mysticism. It was here that music made an unlikely entrance.

The discovery of perspective had a profound impact on the composition of music. Composers of the period were influenced by visual artists' use of perspective. Around 1420 the dukes of Burgundy were taking advantage of the confusion of the Hundred Year's War and the Black Death to run relatively pacific trade fairs. The dukes increased the duchy's commercial viability and visibility by improving the ambience enjoyed by the merchants and traders at these commercial galas. The traders and merchants had disposable income at exactly the time when some itinerant musicians arrived from England with the beginnings of what was to become Franco-Flemish polyphony.

This music caught the ears of the traders and merchants because it was a cultural assault on the traditional, hypnotic plainsong of the Gregorian chants that had been the mainstay of both popular and religious, monastic and lay composition. The Burgundian dukes could see the effect on audiences, and with ducal encouragement, the new music found its audience. With its density and complexity, polyphony seemed to be made for modern men who were pushing the envelope of commerce to its limits.

New composers like Johannes Ockeghem, Josquin, Antoine Brumel, Guillaume Du Fay, Henrich Isaac, Jacob Obrecht, Nicolas Gombert and Jacobus Clemens non Papa seemed destined for top-forty careers. John Dunstable and Leonel Power wrote Masses in the new genre, utilizing familiar chantry sources but blending them throughout with what historians of musicology call Franco-Flemish polyphony. The new music attracted attention from rival trading cities all over Europe.

Other cities of the period began to compete with the duchy for the composers who came to the attention of music scouts of greater patron-rulers. Louis XI of France, Lorenzo the Magnificent of Florence and the Duke of Ferrara each made impressive offers to attract new composers to their courts. Interestingly, the next generation of European composers found the density and abstraction of the Franco-Flemish polyphony too abstract. They returned to fabricating more restful music, leaving the exploration of polyphonic coolness to the twentieth century.

No Lull in the Rush of New Ideas

Ramon Lull (*c.* 1232–1315) was an interesting fellow. He was the most unlikely person you would expect to live to be 93. The spelling of Lull's last name is as varied as most spellings of the period.

We are going to proceed with Lull because of the references to him made by Dr. John Dee, the English magus par excellence. A "magus" was a sixteenth century term for someone who operated on the border of alchemy and science. Hence people saw such a person as a maker of magic and called him a magus. In documents originally found in Dee's Mortlake library, Dee's adversarials on Lull's manuscripts are spelled as "Lull." Adversarials were space on the right hand margin of a book's pages in which the reader would write comments on the text. Dee was well known for his adversarials. Lull's name has been so spelled in English since Dee's time.

Dr. John Dee (c. 1527–1608) was notable as Elizabeth I's court astrologer, physician, alchemist and strategic planner. The truth is that in the 1500s the dividing line between magic and science was very thin and many early historians claimed Dee was mostly a magician. Dee was also the owner of the best library in England and had studied Lull's thinking in Prague, where he had gone to hang out at Charles V's court. This was during a period of Dee's life when his tenure in England was dicey due to allegations having to do with an alleged Protestant plot to poison Mary, Queen of Scots. Dee was an ideological Protestant. He returned to England at the request of Mary's successor, Elizabeth I, who needed him to select the astrologically most propitious time and date for her coronation.

In any event, Ramon Lull began life in Palma, Majorca. As a young man he served in somebody's army during the Hundred Years War, and after the usual Hundred Years War undistinguished military career of general dissoluteness, rape, pillage and looting, he had an epiphanous experience.

In 1266 he applied to the Franciscan monastic order with the intent of becoming a priest. Certainly Lull had an exemplary motivation. He wanted to enter the missionary branch of the order and convert followers of

Islam to Christianity. This was not the best idea the Franciscans had ever heard, but they were accustommed to excessively ambitious ex-soldiers and accepted him with alacrity.

Once he became a *bona fide* Franciscan, Lull turned to asceticism, mortification of the flesh and a general enthusiasm for Franciscan ideals. But years of study had their influence and Lull began to turn out some first-rate thinking. His first notable theological work was the *Ars Magna*. This was nothing less than a primitive logic generator. It was so influential that it came to be known as "the Lullian method." Lull began to gather followers from the ranks of other Franciscan monasteries who started to refer to him as the "enlightened doctor."

To create a logic generator at the end of the thirteenth century was nothing short of true genius. The *Ars Magna* took common spiritual commentaries such as IHS (In His Service) or Aristotle's *Categories* and used them to generate random logical connections from approved sources. But these approved sources would generate previously unknown ideas that could be transferred to new areas of current thought. It is surprising that Lull went uncriticized for these efforts because these new ideas could then influence and stimulate new fields of thought.

The influence of such breakthroughs in fields such as alchemy could have become an attack on the Church's prerogatives as the sole source of knowledge. Amazingly the Church did not recognize the danger this activity posed to its orthodoxy. Lull became a reference point for the beginning of an informed and institutionally unmonitored ideation of both clergy and laity.

After working with his logic generator for a number of years, Lull sailed for Tunis to get to work on his original motivation for entering the priesthood: his project to convert the Islamic faithful in North Africa. This didn't work out too well, as the local Islamic authorities imprisoned him and finally banished him.

He returned to Europe where he visited his followers and supporters in Naples, Rome, Majorca, Cyprus and Armenia. He found that his adherents were actively dabbling in alchemy.

Apparently neither Lull nor the various religious superiors were upset by the Lullists'—as they were calling themselves by that time—interest in alchemy. A small niche coterie of present-day scholars continue to consider Lull as the main line and claim to have proven that Lull himself had nothing to do with the hermetic arts. There is no evidence that anyone else has claimed that Lull was involved with alchemy, so the point is moot. Lull then went on the lecture circuit, challenging the teachings of the noted twelfth century Spanish Islamic philosopher, Ibn Rushd Averroes, as Thomas Aquinas had done in his famous debate with Nicolas of Brabant at the Universty of Paris in 1215.

Lull also wrote much admired poetry which admonished the faithful to avoid impure thoughts as a great danger to one's soul. One such poem features Lust, the main character, following an attractive woman. She leads him into a church and removes her outer garment, revealing that one of her breasts is eaten away with cancer. The poet reminds the reader that it is impure thoughts which have placed Lust in this condition of jeopardizing his soul.

In 1305, Lull went back to the African Mediterranean coastal region, this time to Algeria. Once again he tried to Christianize some Muslims and preached against Averroes, and once again he was busted, banned and deported. In 1315, he returned to Algeria where the Islamic authorities caught him trying to convert the locals to Christianity. As early supporters of the "three strikes and you're out" school of crime prevention, the Islamic authorities in Algeria were miffed, and this time Lull was sentenced to death by stoning, dying a few days later. He finally got his wish, becoming a martyr at 93.

There we have a group of pre-Reformation activists. With the benefit of hindsight we can see that the Church was not filling the revolutionary new needs of the people. Religions are mandated to provide answers to problems that are unknowable and unanswerable. Along the way religions pick up some ancillary functions. Religions are strong in the do-gooder business, the social realm, counseling, psychotherapy, social welfare, education, feeding the poor and promoting the continuity of local customs. When the big questions (Who am I? Why am I here? Why is there war? Why did my child die? Why is my mother sick?) become answerable, and problems become in some way understandable, religions lose a portion of their mandate. Sometimes they accomodate new questions arising from new levels of complexity.

The Renaissance provided the West with a massive shift in world view, including fresh ideas, new perspectives on old ideas, some really ugly wars that went on seemingly interminably and the importance of the idea of intellectual and social stability that had been lost for centuries. And the Renaissance brought along the Reformation as part of the package.

The nation state was born in the Renaissance, and in the West, evolved into the secular nation-state.

Religions became "faith traditions" and offered the state services via "faith-based communities." The anointment of rulers was no longer deemed essential for a government to acquire legitimacy. People, like the ones we have seen in this chapter, laid the groundwork for this new secularism. Religious institutions evolve just as shamans develop specialization and move from gods of varying concrete abilities to single gods whose abilities deal with a broader range of more abstract attributes. Priesthoods, prophecy, augury, medicine, hospices for the sick and education are all examples of the ways in which religious institutional investments make a reformation an awesome prospect not to be undertaken lightly.

A reformation starts out, as we've seen in this chapter, with a significant body of the faithful tweaking the belief system. Sometimes the institutional faith doesn't notice or can't predict the outcome of such tweaking.

The Franco-Flemmish composers who invented new polyphonic music caused an undercutting of the Church's monopoly on institutional music composition and inspired high order mathematics. Ockeghem and the others were not producing "sacred" music, and because they had secular and aristocratic support and no agenda that involved the overthrow of the liturgical Gregorian chant, the Church was unaware and indifferent to the effect of their new music.

The Cathars were a different kind of problem. Although they were eventually violently suppressed by papal armies, they left a legacy of legitimacy of heretical questioning of Church doctrine and dogma that could be picked up by any group that had the courage to act on its beliefs.

Hus and his followers raised challenges across the

whole of the Bohemian countryside, addressing such clear issues as Church ownership of land, whether the Church had the power to issue indulgences and the degree to which it was proper for priests to forgive sins. This revolt in a suburban outport of the Holy Roman Empire required the calling of a full council of the Church in Constance, Switzerland. The council ordered Hus' burning at the stake. The fact that the indulgence issue had the legs to last a century and that Luther picked up on it shows us that the Hus revolt was also a true precursor of the Reformation.

The Hus revolt should have warned the Church, but instead the delegates to the Council at Constance congratulated themselves on stamping out a dangerous heresy. It was their institutional investment that blinded them to what was really going on. Their assumptions about the world meant that they weren't going to get it.

Wycliffe was an example of the pre-Reformation Church's misunderstanding of the way the world and its place in it were changing. Wycliffe was charged by Church inquisitors of publishing the Bible and some religious tracts in vernacular English, not the "universal" Latin. He challenged the Church's authority to grant absolution and deliver indulgences. He called for priests to be subject to secular courts and rules in matters of civil disputes. You may say that Wycliffe was a front man for John of Gaunt and his political ambitions, but his theological ideas would reoccur throughout the next three hundred years.

Looking back on the pre-Reformation period it is hard to imagine that our ancestors did not recognize that a reformation was coming down the track. That is unless they didn't know what a reformation was.

Chapter Two

The Catholics: Church and State—Strangers but Bedfellows

AT THE BEGINNING of the Renaissance (*c.* 1450) the tradition-bound Roman Catholic Church was superficially in very good shape to lead the world into a new period of history. The political structure consisted of two orders which made up the Holy Roman Empire: the Catholic Church and the secular states that comprised the empire.

Leadership of the Church was vested in the pope who was and is in the present, elected for life by the College of Cardinals in a sacred conclave. The pope was responsible for controlling matters religious, moral and spiritual.

The secular side of the Holy Roman Empire was led by a Holy Roman Emperor who was elected by feudal lord peers. The emperor exercised less disciplined control over the lords. Each emperor was chosen from among the elector lords and it was required that he be anointed with oil by the pope or a papal legate at his coronation. Anointment was a significant act, it joined the Church and the state together in a mystical relationship.

This left little doubt which group held the upper hand. The lords spiritual, the cardinals and bishops were constitutionally far superior to the lords temporal by virtue of the need for anointment of the emperor by the pope or his emissary.

The emperor was sworn at his coronation to uphold and defend the Church. His anointment in holy oil by the Church through its papal agent was evidence of his feudal obligation to the Church and the pope. This made the mystical union of anointment between the emperor and God one that was mediated by the Church. Hence, the Church was the guarantor of the emperor's good faith as well was the beneficiary of the state's willingness to protect, with force of arms if need be, the Church's rights and privileges.

Needless to say this state of affairs led to a high level of corruption becoming rampant in the Church, with bishoprics and cardinalships being regularly sold along with anything else that wasn't nailed down.

The lords temporal were equally concerned with cutting corners. Every so often a strong regional ruler would come along and if he had a big enough army, or the assets to borrow money for mercenaries, he could exert lots of influence on the electors or simply invade other states and become the next Holy Roman Emperor.

As the Renaissance moved along all of this abuse of power began to have a negative impact on the new middle class. These people were the ones who were using new ideas and inventions to build new economies. These new economies were based on trade and took advantage of the increased movement of agricultural workers to the cities every time a new plague or natural disaster struck, or there was an economic shift such as growth of the shipping industry.

The Church was also in control of the universities,

which were the fonts for all the new earth-shaking ideas that we call the Renaissance. Pre-Renaissance universities were run under a system called scholasticism. A scholastic environment was very much like the Islamic schools of today (the Madrasses). The lecturer would read texts by either the Fathers of the Church, or the adopted fathers who were pre-Christian Romans and Greeks. The students would memorize what was read to them in the lectures. Until the invention of printing there was a great shortage of textbooks and library facilities, so the lectures were largely oral in nature.

After the invention of print technology in the 1450s, printing quickly moved throughout Europe and a new generation of academics, called humanists, began to take over the universities. This new generation of scholars resisted or re-examined and refuted most scholastic thought and assumptions. These humanists, like the Italian poet Petrarch, were the source of much of the support for the Reformation.

As the Church's corruption grew, there was an unwillingness among the hierarchy to examine new ideas, except for purposes of refutation. The Church perceived itself as being flooded with questioning of its doctrine and dogma, as well as by opposition to its more conventional varieties of corruption (such as the sale of indulgences). It moved swiftly to eradicate these ideas often by crying heresy. For example, the contemporary authority on anatomy and physiology was a Greek named Galen. Galen had been born in Asia Minor in AD 130. He moved to Smyria, (currently Syria) Corinth and Alexandria where he studied medicine. He was, among other things, the chief physician to the gladiators of Pergamum. He then moved to Rome, where he became the friend of and physician to the Roman emperor Marcus Aurelius. Obviously no fault was found with Galen's treatment because after Marcus Aurelius' death, Galen continued as physician to his son, the new Emperor Commodus and to his successor, the Emperor Severus.

In addition to his thriving medical practice, Galen was a prolific author, writing treatises on medicine and 15 papers on the thought of Hypocrites. There are 83 extant documents of authenticated Galen authorship that have survived to the present. Unfortunately, in the area of anatomy and physiology Galen performed dissections only on animals. He was the first to use the pulse as a diagnostic tool.

Among Galen's many bright ideas was the idea that women were frequent sufferers from hysteria because the uterus had no permanent location but floated all over the interior of the torso. Its principal function was to devour sperm. There is no evidence that Galen did any dissections on humans. He drew all his anatomical knowledge by inference from his animal studies.

The Church not only held Galen's theories to be sacrosanct but outlawed anatomical dissection of human cadavers. Medical autopsy was illegal, but was performed nonetheless as an underground activity. Then Andreas Vesalius (1514–1564), a Flemish anatomist, came along and proceeded not only to do autopsies on human cadavers, but to employ an artist to illustrate these dissections in all the accuracy and illustrative clarity the newly discovered perspective allowed.

Vesalius' drawings and his descriptions of the anatomical dissections were published in *De humani corporis fabrica* (1543) with the new print technology, permitting mass distribution. When this happened, the Church took the matter in hand by calling in the

Inquisition. The inquisitors found Vesalius to be a heretic, and a repudiator of Galenism. He was sentenced to death by burning at the stake, for "body snatching."

Grave robbing or buying bodies from the families of those who had been executed was not an unusual practice among medical students and humanist professors of medicine in search of bodies to examine. Vesalius was able to circumvent execution only because he was the physician to the court of Philip II of Castile. Even so, in a plea bargain by Philip, Vesalius was forced to undertake a pilgrimage to Jerusalem as an alternative to his death sentence. While returning from this pilgrimage he became ill and died in Asia Minor, attended to probably by a Galenist.

The wars of the Renaissance were fought over religion thinly disguised as political ideology. While today we can only shake our heads in disbelief at the Vesalius episode, it was a relatively common event, as was his crime. Vesalius was convicted because body theft and autopsy was entirely too common in Europe's humanist universities, and he made a good example. He was prominent, he was refuting Galen—a Father of the Church—which meant heresy, and he was holding the Church up to disrepute. He was also questioning the Church's ability to legislate truth and to justify its universalist character.

The Inquisitor's Dilemma

In 1233 Gregory IX was elected pope and within a year felt the time was ripe to elevate one Dominic de

Guzmin to sainthood. This was a little curious because Dominic had only been dead since 1221 and had had a strange career prior to becoming a saint.

Dominic had been an unimportant monk when he met the bishop of Osma during the crusade against the Cathars. He was filled with outraged indignation at the heretical activities of the Cathars and offered to organize a group of itinerant monks to oppose them on the ground where the Cathars were strongest. The Cathars were particularly effective preachers, so Dominic's monks and friars could not be sequestered in order houses but would need to be unfettered so they could go and oppose any Cathar-based heresies where they popped up.

Dominic himself was a messianic-messenger type of person. He lived a frugal life, never sleeping in a bed but only on the ground, or on a board if he was staying in an inn. He wore a hair shirt under his habit and frequently whipped himself with chains that he kept wrapped around his legs for that very purpose. It was said that when he was to stay in an inn he would first drink his fill from a nearby spring or stream so as not to be tempted by the pleasure of the inn's wine or beer.

During the battles with the Cathars, Dominic was always in the front ranks of the anti-Cathar crusaders, right beside the papal legate, Arnald-Amaury, abbot of Citeaux, who frequently ordered the execution of whole communities and was the originator of the saying "God will recognize His own."

After the Crusade Dominic recognized that the fine body of men he had moulded might be better employed if they were in a recognized order. The Fourth Lateran Council held in 1215 provided Dominic with the chance to lobby Pope Innocent III about establishing the order to be called the Dominican order. The pope said it was okay with him, but before the paper work could be processed he died. In 1216, Pope Honorius was elected, and he fullfilled Innocent's pledge to Dominic. The Dominican order was in business. The first Dominican order house was established in France in Toulouse. Dominic got busy selling the hair shirt idea, the self-flagellation regimen and giving public lectures. The Dominicans monks and friars were soon giving the local parish priests and bishop, monks and friars in other orders so much attitude about how the Dominicans were purer than everyone else, that they were driven out of town.

In 1221, Dominic died of some unidentified fever in Bologna. Before his death, his true-believer strategy had produced twenty Dominican order houses in France and Spain. For example, in 1224, there were over 120 Dominicans in Paris alone studying theology at the university.

Field work was not left fallow and bishops and cardinals were finding out that if you had a heresy problem in your diocese, the Dominicans were the ones to call. Outstanding preachers, aggressive theologians and unrelenting heretic hunters, the Dominicans were even attracting the pope's eye.

Pope Gregory IX, who had canonized Dominic, had a mission for the Dominicans. He published a papal bull in 1233 instructing the Dominicans to establish a tribunal for rooting out heresy wherever it appeared. Unsatisfied with that bull, Pope Gregory issued a second bull two days later authorizing the Dominicans to call on secular forces if they ran into any problems enforcing the first bull. Any lord temporal or any local ruler feudally obligated to the lord who didn't assist the

Dominicans in their fight against heresy was now placing the lord temporal's anointment oath at risk.

The institutional Inquisition took some more time to become established, but the pro forma authority was now there. The Church's ability to self-correct or respond to social and intellectual shifts had a huge constitutional and psychological barrier placed in its path. On the other hand, a vehicle had been acquired by the Church that enabled it to address any troublemakers against whom a heresy case could be made to stick. This version of the Inquisition was put into practice most famously when the Church found two new targets: demons and Jews.

Let's take note of the demons first. Father Abba Poemen, a hermit priest who became a Father of the Church, wrote in regard to the nature of demons, "It is from our own wills that become the demons and it is these that attack us." Later churchmen had found that demons could pass between walls and even through locked doors. The clergy discovered that a regular part of their pastoral duties was the trade of casting out demons.

In 1484, Pope Innocent VIII expressed profound concern over demons and was determined to do something about the problem, which by then was wreaking havoc all over Europe. To accomplish this he published a bull, which said in part

> It has come to Our attention that members of both sexes have intercourse with evil angels, incubi and succubi, and that by their sorceries, and by their incantations, charms and conjurations, they suffocate, extinguish, and cause to perish the births of women.

Two Dominican friars, Henry Kramer and James Sprenger, were appointed as Apostolic legates and inquisitors to conduct a commission of inquiry into the heresies involved in demonology and witchcraft.

In 1478 the Castilian (or Spanish) Inquisition was established. After the Islamic expulsion in Castile, all of the Jews in Castile were required to convert to Christianity. By 1492 there were some questions about the sincerity of these conversions. In 1502 Muslims were forced to accept the Catholic faith, and the Inquisition went all out to inquire into the validity of their conversions. The usual methods of inquiry were employed by the inquisitors—torture, burning at the stake—but a new one made its appearance. Most of the Jews and Muslims were allowed to make large donations to the Church before being expelled to North Africa. Jews and Muslims who could not make a significant donation were able to contribute by being tortured or killed, thus providing encouragement to those who could raise funds to do so with alacrity.

When the Protestant Reformation came along with its many sidebar wars, Protestants who were captured found themselves facing the same Inquisitorial charges already tested on the Jews and Muslims. In addition, English and Dutch Protestant sailors were routinely sold as galley slaves to the North African Muslims.

Meanwhile, on the demons and witches fronts, Kramer and Sprenger returned a report known as the *Malleus Maleficarum*. It is a document of awesome proportions that sets out how to capture those who are possessed by demons and those who are witches. Kramer and Sprenger began with the biblical injunction, "Thou Shalt not suffer a witch to live." This, of course, poses the problem, "That's all very well, but how do you tell who is a witch and who isn't? And how do you tell who is possessed by a demon?"

To this Kramer and Spengler responded, "Torture. That's the only sure method to prove witchcraft." They also thought favourably of having witches or demon-carriers who had confessed identify other witches or demonists. Then the inquisitors recommended that the civil tribunals, who by Church law had to order the execution, should be paid an emolument for each confessed witch. The cost of an expert torturer was to be borne by the prisoner. The prisoner was also responsible for paying for the stake, rope, wood, pitch and other combustables necessary for the successful community entertainment known as burning at the stake.

Other costs were also charged to the accused or their estate, including fees for bounty hunters, informers and guards. Seldom was anyone indicted by the Inquisition and then found innocent. The Inquisition operated all over Europe and accompanied the Spanish and Portuguese to the colonies in America and Asia.

The Inquisition acted as the enforcement arm of the Church. It became another area of the Church's corruption to cause outrage among the clerical leaders of the Reformation when the movement got underway in Europe.

The state leaders of the Protestant cause became more and more convinced that they could find a better use for feudal financial obligations and religious tithes. Certainly a far better use than the Church or its feudal lords temporal and their foreign exchange reserves would swell exponentially.

He Kept a Diary

Another figure you won't find in your high school history text on the Reformation is a bureaucrat named
Johann Burchard. He was a German born in Haslach,
became a friar and went to the Vatican as a young man
in 1481. He was spotted as an administrative bright one
and became the papal master of ceremonies two years
later. He was the ceremonial chief to the first Borgia
pope, Alexander VI. Alexander VI was the father of a
daughter, Lucrezia Borgia, and a son, Cesare, whom he
made a cardinal at eighteen. Alexander's idea was to
install a hereditary papacy.

Not only was he Alexander's Master of Ceremonies,
but he kept a diary! A few hundred years later the diary
was found in the Vatican Library and published for
scholarly distribution in Latin. In 1963 the Folio Society
of London released a translation, edited by Geoffrey
Parker, under the title *At the Court of the Borgias*. From
this diary we learn the day-to-day details of a
Pontificate reputed to be the most corrupt and criminal
papacy in the fifteenth century or since.

Burchard's Diary had been held originally in the
Vatican Library's "Not for Circulation" collection and
was unquestionably written as a private memoria of his
years in the papal service. Indeed Burchard, who was
the most discrete of men, would have been shocked to
think that it would be published. The diary contains
Burchard's notes on the order of precedence and other
preparations for public ceremonies as would befit a
bureaucrat for whom carrying out the details to perfection was a matter of pride. The normal course of his
duties required that he understand the dynamics of

court intrigues so he might account for them as an event manager.

It was also necessary that he keep aware of the pope's intentions in matters diplomatic and administrative. Interestingly, Burchard began the diary concerned only with the propriety of his office, but a change soon came over him as he became aware of the total corruption, double-dealing, court-arranged murders, private lives of the pope, his children and their half-brothers and sisters who also inhabited the papal apartments. Knowing about a court conspiracy to commit a murder was one thing; arranging the funeral of the victim—in which the pope and the official Vatican community were expected to participate—required Burchard to develop a flexibility unanticipated by most bureaucrats.

The final figure that we must look at to understand the failure of the Church to adapt to the intellectual and social changes that brought about the Reformation is Giordano Bruno (1548–1600). Bruno was probably the finest mind of the Renaissance, but he is better known as the Dominican friar who fell into disrepute with his Dominican Order superiors.

Originally from Naples, Bruno first worked at a few second-rate teaching jobs in Naples and Paris, teaching philosophy at the baccalaureate level. In 1583, he was recommended by the king of France, Henri III, with whom he had become friendly, to the French ambassador to England, Michel de Castelnau, seigneur de Mauvissiere. The idea was that he become the chaplain at the French embassy in London.

De Castelnau was a devout Catholic as was his wife Marie Bochetel, who was about 30 years younger than the ambassador. She was the heiress of a distinguished, wealthy and very Catholic family who, for generations, had loyally served French royalty in many capacities. De Castelnau was engaged in activities designed to secure the escape of Mary, Queen of Scots from the jail where she had been incarcerated for plotting the assassination of her half-sister Elizabeth I.

The ambassador, who spoke English fluently, considered himself a friend and cultural admirer of England. The only thing to mar this ideal was that de Castelnau hated Protestants even more than his wife did. He blamed the Huguenots (the French Protestants) for the ravages France had suffered in the Thirty Years War. He was not kindly disposed to Huguenot refugees who had escaped to England. England was a posting he delighted in for the social amenities. Unfortunately England was a very Protestant country.

Sir Francis Walsingham, the British secretary of state for foreign affairs and head of the English secret service, was deeply concerned about de Castelnau's plotting around Mary. He managed to recruit Bruno as an English spy under the code name of Henry Fagot. Bruno performed admirably. No spymaster could have asked for a better agent than Bruno. Tireless in hearing confessions, attending Madame de Castelnau's teas and other social gatherings, Bruno assiduously noted the names of all the Englishmen who sneaked into the embassy to plot with de Castelnau for Elizabeth's overthrow and Mary's return to the throne. Bruno made copious notes about what they and the ambassador said. It was Bruno who fingered the leader of the Throckmorton plot[1], and when Walsingham's intelligencers drew in that net, it made Catholic plots in England a thing of the past for a generation.

The interesting thing about all of this was that when the Inquisition questioned Bruno many years later, it was interested in a book he had written called *Shadows of Ideas*. In the book, Bruno had expressed the idea that in light of Copernicus' discovery, a new epistemology was evidently needed. The Inquisition was interested in the cosmology that he was promoting and wanted to know whether, when he was in England, he had ever heard confessions or granted the sacraments while his preaching license was suspended. They were not interested at all in whether he might be a Walsingham spy, only whether he had contaminated the ambassador with his unorthodox religious views. After three years of interrogation, Bruno was executed.

This was at the end of the sixteenth century when almost all of Europe was engaged in the wars of the Reformation. Because the inquisitors were looking in the wrong place for the wrong things, Henry Fagot would go free and Giordano Bruno would go to the stake. Although Bruno was never recorded as having even a fleeting interest in things Protestant, the Inquisition missed the chance to test any of his thoughts because they were seen as heretical

Chapter Three

The Protestants

AS WE HAVE seen, Protestantism had its beginnings in an attempt to reform the established Church. In Chapter One we saw that there were a number of issues floating around, including willingness to engage in heresy (or what the Church chose to suppress as heresy) and questioning of doctrine and dogma that cried out for some measure of reform. There were three sectors of societ—the aristocracy, the reformists and clergy—which were on separate tracks, all bent on adapting to the changes brought on by the Renaissance.

The Renaissance triggered a big change in the world view of Western countries. It wasn't by any means a coherent shift in the major assumables of the peoples of Western Europe. Still, over the next few hundred years, the new values implicit in the Renaissance crystalized into, first the Mercantile Age, then the Age of Reason and then the beginning of the industrial era.

There were radical changes that came out of the Renaissance which eventually affected everyone. One change was that the nation state evolved and became the secular nation state. The followers of the Protestant Reformation shook themselves loose from the feudal obligations of the Holy Roman Empire. The feudal obligations of the pre-Renaissance became looser.

Serfdom became less of an inescapable bondage as cities grew and serfs escaped their rural bondage in times of plague, drought, war or simply as economic refugees (to use today's parlance). Some jobs, outside of the army and diplomatic missions, already required mobility.

The mason's guild, for example, had houses modelled after monastic order houses in every European city where there was a building boom. These masonic lodges provided a base for the organization of workers—outside of the manorial economy—who had a trade as masons. Soon other artisan guilds followed suit. The law officers of cities were less than likely to enforce the return of manorial escapers to their feudal lords. Plague or other natural events placed labour availability at a premium. The new cities were as short of labour as the rural areas—if not more so—and were building new economies and offering new opportunities. The cities offered economic inducements attracting former rural workers. Agents of the nobility would find little cooperation in their attempts to return runaway serfs to the manorial estate. Cities were growing both physically and in terms of population. These expanding cities had an economic need for an increased work force. The new industrial factories required housing for masses of workers. This need created a tension between the new economy and the dominant manorial economy.

This widespread new mobility was one cause of the emergence of a new middle class. Many people took advantage of improved technology and work opportunities to exercise the options that were becoming available, in order to achieve social and economic mobility.

When Geoffrey Chaucer (c. 1342-1400) wrote *The Canterbury Tales*, he documented this movement in the "Prologue" to the *Tales*. The *Tales* tell the story of a group of medieval people (a prioress, a nun, a knight, a priest, a monk, an almoner and other typical residents of fourteenth century England) on a pilgrimmage to the shrine at Canterbury Cathedral. These people were what we might call middle class, except that the term did not exist back then. What is interesting about the *Tales* is that the characters are presented as pretty ordinary people even though most medieval historians tell us that the average person at that time spent their entire life not travelling more than fifty miles from their place of birth and then only in exceptional circumstances. So Chaucer was promoting the idea of mobility and social class interaction. He himself had travelled as far as Prague on diplomatic missions.

Christianity represented a massive shift in the culture of the world. In most of the world's other religions, there is a way to adapt to an enduring fatalism. Christianity broke from this all-encompassing fatalism and carried instead a message of evangelical hope. If you are in the midst of a plague and most of the world says "It is our fate" or "It's God's will" or "The gods are angry with us and are exacting punishment" or "There is nothing we can do," there is little inducement to find the cause, and eventually a cure, for the epidemic. In contrast, a post-Renaissance culture first says "Let us discover a way to discover the cause of events" and invents a scientific method. Then an interlocutory device is developed in order to ask "What caused the plague?" or whatever event is killing or otherwise inconveniencing the population. When the cause is found, the culture discovers that to use the "fate" model does not provide a useful explanatory model to search out causality, or more recently, functional relationships.

The reason the established church mishandled all

the change vectors was that it had no way to accommodate massive shifts of world view. When the social zeitgeist undergoes a reordering and that reordering destabilizes the established order, the establishment isn't going to give up its benefits to be part of an unknown new world. It either goes into denial or brings out the army. Either way, it isn't going to give up all the perks of being the establishment voluntarily.

The Big Players

In the beginning there were genuine religious reformers, some of whom we have already met in Chapter One. It happens pretty simply. A theologian, or a religious fanatic, or a zealot, or a logician, or a person with a vision questions Church doctrine on something. It can be indulgences, priestly power to dispense forgiveness for sins, bishops who are aping the rights of secular rulers' penchant for material goods, land acquisitions or the papal governance breakdown. If the message strikes a chord among the populace, the reformers attract a following. In the early days the message had to be simple because complexity wouldn't bring in the followers. Otherwise you need some really strong and convincing preachers like the Cathars had. You also need a strong case of zealotry among the followers.

Let's also understand that the established Church had no interest whatsoever in giving the reformers a fair hearing. History tells us that where most reformers end up is as guests of the secret police (The Inquisition), the Star Court Chamber—the Protestant incarnation of The Inquisition, or else opposing a numerically and weapons-superior army, or getting caught in a civil war. In the Thirty Years War, (a.k.a. "The Wars of Religion") the French civil and clerical establishments chose to see the country decimated rather then grant any rights to the Huguenots or allow free choice in religious matters. The Huguenots were the incipient middle class in France. Civil wars are the bloodiest, most destructive of war mankind has so far invented, and the Protestant Reformation generated more than its share of civil wars.

The other thing that you have to remember is that for a reform movement to succeed it must recruit representative members of the secular ruling powers. In the case of the Reformation, Martin Luther and John Calvin would not have achieved very much had they not established firm alliances with some of the civil authorities. The leaders of the Reformation were pretty hard-nosed people. Calvin, Luther and John Knox (the founder of the Presbyterian Church in Scotland) needed the aid of the leaders of states to establish secure bases from which to work.

England's Henry VIII (1491–1547) was probably the handsomest, most accomplished and most intellectual ruler and politician in Europe. He had been tutored by Sir Thomas More and Desidarius Erasmus of Rotterdam. After establishing alliances with convenient rulers in Europe, only to break them off soon after, Henry prepared, with the aid of his prelate statesman, Thomas Wolsey, to launch a plan that was truly audacious.

The plan was that England would become the balance of power between France and Spain. Given England's meagre assets, entitlement to a role as arbiter between the great powers would have been a less than likely event under more conventional circumstances.

The scheme called for an end-game where England became an absolute monarchy. Henry pulled off the greatest piece of diplomatic legerdemain ever when, on getting a copy of Luther's 95 theses, he published a personal reply. His exceptional book on the sacraments was widely and favourably received by Church theologians. Since Henry VIII's criticism of Luther was rigorous and telling, as well as being theologically competent, Pope Leo X saw his alliance with Henry as one of the better deals of his pontificate. After all, most of the princes Leo had to deal with had trouble writing their own name and spelling it the same way twice in a row. Henry had written a well-argued theological treatise that hit Martin Luther in his expansive underbelly. This alliance was between the pope, Francis I of France and Henry VIII. The deal was that Francis would do any fighting that was necessary and the pope and Henry would be his non-fighting friends. Then Henry started his own national church. Then the pope anathematised Henry.

Poor Leo. In his unthinking gratitude, he not only wrote letters of endearment to Henry but awarded both Henry and his heirs the inheritable title of "Defender of the Faith." Even after the inevitable breach with the papacy occurred and Henry had established the Church of England, he continued to hold on to this title. His lawful heir, Elizabeth II, the reigning monarch, questioned allowing the annointment part of her coronation to be televised in 1952 because it would expose the mystical aspect of the coronation to public scrutiny. Elizabeth II never once considered not being annointed, so to this day she is an annointed monarch. Her successor will also be annointed— if she has anything to say about her successor's coronation—and she has lots to say about it.

Another Renaissance character who requires mention if we want to understand how lacking in fun a reformation would be is Girolamo Savonarola (1452–1498). Savonarola was a religious and political reformer. He is the template against whom all zealots, right up to the present time, have to test their claim to the title. Born into a noble family in Ferrara, Italy and signed on with the Dominicans, of whom we spoke earlier, Savonarola was sent to Florence in Italy where a humanist explosion of art and literature had occurred under the patronage of Lorenzo de Medici. His first preaching assignment was considered a failure, and his lack of enthusiasm for the Florentine brand of humanism was commented upon. It was obvious to his superiors that Savonarola wasn't ready for prime time. He was sent to a convent in Brescia that needed to be shaken up. All accounts of his ministry to the convent seem to mention the word "zeal" or "zealous" or "zealotry," and in some unfriendly sources the word "fanatic" is even used.

To his Dominican superiors this suggested that their system was working and their original faith in Savonarola was justified. He had just needed some time in the minors to get on his feet. When Savonarola was sent back to Florence, he was pretty much a fire-and-brimstone preacher expressing negative views about the humanists. Then in 1493 there was a political upheaval within the Dominican order and Savonarola was named vicar-general of the order. From this point on, Savonarola became more of a political revolutionary, preaching about changes in government based on his own strained theology, which called for reformation of religion and morality to come to a political state that would portend a time of God's will being done by man. This resulted in him being completely on the outs with

Lorenzo de Medici's successors. Savonarola's response was to predict the imminent arrival of God's messenger in the form of France's Charles VIII and his French army as the head of the divinely inspired state.

Lo and behold, Charles did come to Florence. Unfortunately for Savonarola's prophetic reputation, Charles and his French army were soon forced out of the city, leaving Savonarola to discuss predictions and fraternizing with the enemy with the city's Medici leaders. Somehow Savonarola got out of this embarrasing bind and all agreed that Florence should become a Christian commonwealth with Savonarola as the guiding light. His newly organized political party, called the "Weepers," came out the winners from the post-French chaos.

Savonarola invented an unusual form of Catholic puritanism calling for suppression of vice and corruption as well as the outlawing of gambling and the banning of vain apparel. He held a big demonstration and demanded that the most arrogant clothes horses in town had to offer up their wardrobes and accessories to a huge bonfire which Savonarola dubbed "The Bonfire of the Vanities," which Tom Wolfe would recycle and use as the title for his *fin de siecle* novel about late-twentieth-century Wall Street excesses. By now Savonarola was making doom-laden prophecies about imminent disaster events to everyone who didn't get it for his doom scenarios which he preached to massive crowds.

Soon he was called to Rome to answer charges of heresy based on his prophetic pronouncements. Obviously Savonarola was much too busy and too important to deal with a little thing like a heresy charge, and when he didn't show up, the Inquisition pulled his license to preach. Anyone could see that this was all a little weird. Savonarola was, after all, the vicar-general of the Dominicans and the Inquisition was made up of fellow Dominicans. In 1497 the pope excommunicated Savonarola, effectively barring him from all priestly duties. The Franciscans and the Dominicans set to work to destroy his reputation, though the Franciscans were more interested in dissing the Dominicans as a group. During a plague epidemic in 1498, Savonarola took time off from the hell and damnation preaching and cared for monks who came down with the plague like a good Christian father should. He also held another Bonfire of the Vanities.

In 1498 the Medici party recovered the government of Florence and Savonarola was brought to trial, charged with having claimed to see visions, uttering prophecies, expounding religious error and finally, sedition. The finding of guilt by the court was a foregone conclusion, so Savonarola and two Dominican followers were hanged and burned at the stake, all the time declaring their loyalty to the Catholic Church. To this day Savonarola is claimed by some historians as a forerunner of the Reformation. He was certainly a man who took advantage of the collapsing medieval world order to impose his own fanaticism on a small corner of the Renaissance that wasn't quite ready to reject that kind of charisma.

That gives you another glimpse of the world of the Reformation. Naturally the Church wasn't going to admit that its governing procedures were less than outstanding, so it launched the counter-reformation. The result was more bloodshed all over Europe. By that time, however, the Protestant Reformation had secured itself in Northern Europe, large sections of Germany, the Dutch part of Holland and in England. Both the Orthodox and Roman Catholic parts of Europe held the remainder. The Protestant reform movement was the religious and political home of the new middle class and inspired the term "Protestant work ethic" to be added to the lexicon. It also found a place in the Puritan codex as an identifier of one whom God had elected for salvation.

Another event that was to affect Western Europe and North America was the rise of the Puritan movement. Puritans believed that salvation only came about by faith and God's election. Good works were not enough; a strong religious life would not ensure that you were entitled to a place with the heavenly host; only by faith alone could salvation be achieved. God would choose only those whose faith was absolute. It was hard to tell whom God had chosen since the traditional tests didn't have much predictive value. You could do all the good works you wanted, but unless your faith caused God to select you to go into heaven with Him, all the good works were of no avail. The only thing you knew was that the elect maxed out on good works, and good works without faith were a sign of nothing. Similarly, God would imbue the elect with all the piety any one could want, so unless your religious faith came from God, no matter how pious your demeanour, it would not influence the probability of your salvation.

Chapter Four

The Protestant Reformation's
Accomplishments

THE ACCOMPLISHMENTS OF the Protestant Reformation were quite significant. It created a new social and political framework that was attuned to emerging political, intellectual and economic events. It was also amenable to the fine-tuning of religious mantras so as not to unduly inhibit the new science that was emerging.

Savonarola, Bruno and Galileo were victims of an absolutist papacy, its institutional bureaucracy and the Holy Roman Empire. Isaac Newton and John Locke enjoyed the king of England's favour and the freedom to publish. (There is no need to recall here the claims of plagiarism by Leibniz or the mathematical errors peppering Newton's *Principia Mathematica*.) The point is that the Catholic Inquisition was held in high odium in Protestant countries, and while the English Star Court Chamber was every bit as nasty, the activities of that court were confined pretty much to sedition—even when couched in religious terms.

The Spill-over of the Reformation: Divine Right of Kings

France fought with its domestic Protestants after Calvin

had preached reformation to the populace. The Huguenots had been drawn to a reformational view by Calvin or priests whom Calvin had influenced. The Huguenots were mostly drawn from a newly mobile artisan class and *rentier* minor aristocrats. The artisans had trade skills that included inventing new technologies to accommodate a burgeoning economy. On St. Bartholomew's Day, 1572, forces of the duke of Guise on orders of Charles IX of France initiated a massacre wiping out the Parisian Huguenots and driving large numbers of French Protestant survivors out of the country as refugees. A favourite destination for the Huguenots was England.

The French monarchs had been encouraged by their advisors to strive for absolutist rule. This absolute course of action was proposed initially by Cardinal Richelieu. In due course Richelieu mentored a successor, Jules Mazarin, an Italian who, for a brief time, was a layman until Richelieu put him on fast track to becoming a cardinal. Then another advisor succeeded Mazarin.

This was Jean Baptiste Colbert, after whom the current French system of government—Colbertism—is named. Every year the Ecole Nationale d'Administration in Paris recruits 200 elite students to provide the top government and business leaders of the future. If you are recruited, your future is very sweet indeed. One of the bars at the Ecole, some would say the only bar, is whether the student has been sufficiently infused with the spirit of Colbertism to qualify as a graduate: does the student understand the necessity for a profoundly centralized government and the need for everyone who is a true insider to support such a forcefully centralizing government?

Before the advent of Richelieu, France had one of the better consultative assemblies in Europe. Known as the Estates General, it had attempted a minor reform of government in 1643. Such a reform was not in the cards, however, for the absolutist plans of Richelieu, Mazarin and Colbert. That year, the Estates General was dismissed by Louis XIV and not recalled until the French Revolution of 1789. France became a full-fledged, absolutist monarchy. Until that point France had not only an inclusive, functioning national assembly but working provincial assemblies and even serviceable municipal councils.

The Estates General had three different parts representing three classes of the societ: the aristocrats, the clergy and the bourgeoisie. France was very close to becoming the big winner in the Renaissance sweepstakes, but the Wars of Religion took the national attention away from understanding the Reformation forces that were at work.

In England James I succeeded Elizabeth and the Stuart reign began. James was every bit as much a fan of absolute monarchical rule as were the French crowned heads. In fact James and other English proponents of absolutism wrote a number of political tracts that were published on the continent. (That is, beside his well known *Blaste Against Tobacco*.) And foreign absolutist promoters such as St. Bede, John Barclay and Jean Bodin were, in turn, published in England. While the French were successful in establishing rule guided by the divine rule of kings, the Stuarts failed in their attempts to impose a similar regime in England. After all, the example of the beheaded Charles I was a lesson the Stuarts did not need to learn again. England in a Cromwellian civil war is a less than pretty sight.

We're talking here about a monarchy unfettered by restraints. The idea was that the ruler was appointed by God and could not be limited by constraints imposed by his subjects. The monarch would not be limited in his actions by any agency of government. In both countries the support for an absolutist crown came largely from a powerfully connected clergy. Certainly there had been support for the absolute point of view as far back as the Tudor reigns of Elizabeth I and Henry VIII.

Examples in support of English absolutism come from both Protestants and Catholics in the first half of the sixteenth century. On the Protestant side we have William Tyndale, the Bible translator, while a decidedly Catholic view comes from the polemicist Stephen Gardiner. As the Reformation continued, constitutional issues became more frequently couched in religious arguments. In 1789 France had a full-scale revolution that was filled with metaphors. These metaphorical events only confused the revolutionary goals.

Arguments for and against absolutism in England straddled the Protestant–Catholic dividing line. Protestant England feared that the Stuarts—James I, Charles I and Charles II—wanted to abandon the common law of England and make their own wishes or ruling whims superior to the common law. In opposition, the Protestant leaders couched their arguments against the absolutist arguments in religious terms, supporting their position with quotations from scriptures. They also used analogies and pointed remarks about James' and Charles I's Catholicism. The absolutists, on the other hand, asserted that a king had to be prepared to change plans as the situation required. This view was supported by purely rational arguments, derived from natural and constitutional law.

The compatibility of the Protestant movement with the new nation-state and new merchant class (who were a large componant of the the religious reformists) meant that the great new trading companies resident in Holland and England, whose ships were engaged in expansion of trade, made these countries wealthy, the true inheritors of the Reformation. The British East India Company, the Muscovy Company, and the Hudson's Bay Company were all founded by active Protestants. The Muscovy Company provides us with a good look at a market economy in full swing.

There had been an idea floating around since the time of Henry VIII that a Northwest Passage to Kathai (China) would be a good idea and there was a lot of activity around this core thought. John Dee was involved with the scheme, and in the course of getting explorers to find the Northwest Passage, another plan surfaced. Adrian Gilbert suggested that a company be formed to trade into Muscovy (present-day Russia).

Adrian Gilbert was a well-connected merchant trader in London and the brother of the pirate, ship's captain and Arctic explorer Sir Humphrey Gilbert. Dee procured rutters[2] that belonged to the Hanseatic League which gave the Muscovy ships access to the Baltic ports and, therefore, into Muscovy itself. This cut out the odious middle-men in the access to the Muscovy trade. By cutting out the middlemen, Gilbert and Dee planned to triple their profits. Having secured for the Muscovy Company the rutters to the Baltic ports, the company's ships were able to get to the shores and ports of Muscovy such as St. Petersburg. The British ambassador to Ivan the Terrible's court was then able to procure a licence for the company to trade into the inland cities of Muscovy itself, down the Volga and even into the Orient. Thus these traders were no longer restricted to the port cities and had bypassed a host of middlemen. In its first year of operation the Muscovy Company showed a net return on investment of 500 percent.

When you compare the investment of the Muscovy Company with the commercial operations of the French in North America, you see a huge difference in style. In New France the right to trade in either direction for all commercial ventures was held by a foundation called the Company of One Hundred Associates, controlled by—who else—Jean Baptiste Colbert. This monopoly was empowered by a royal charter and payed only a substantial one-time fee to the French king. Naturally this set-up was an impediment to colonial development since the Company of One Hundred Associates had no incentive to build up the colony. An absolute monarchy that charges for monopolies often gives no thought to capital appreciation. Colbert thought he could collect the one-time exorbitant fee for the king, collect the monopoly for his court associates, and then as a result, the colonists in New France and the consumers of the colonists' exports in France would pay outrageous prices.

On the other hand, the English king's role in the Muscovy Company was as an investor. Unfortunately for Adrian Gilbert, John Dee, the king of England and the rest of the investors, after an auspicious start-up, some of Ivan's court intrigued against the Muscovy Company. Given Ivan's reputation for inflicting bodily pain, the company's managers in Muscovy were happy to be expelled only. Shortly thereafter, the company's operations in Muscovy were closed down.

The British needed revenue and it was their trading

companies that showed massive returns on investment. The British East India Company was trading in spices from the Banda Islands just to the south of New Guinea. The return on investment for nutmeg, for example, was greater than what could be obtained from a comparable weight in gold. The nutmeg trade was only a small part of the revenue of the British East India Company. The basic goal of the British was for trading companies to build an asset base, whereas absolutist governments like the French needed immediate cash to pay for the court and clergy requirements. The French merchant traders, for example, had to pay the missionary expenses for the Jesuit order and the Sulpician order.

In the post-Reformation period, Europe saw the founding of a number of scientific societies. These societies were both formal and informal. The impact of these societies was a huge cross-fertilization of ideas. Because there wasn't a large number of people involved, someone interested in a particular problem or in a discipline could readily reach out and touch a kindred spirit. The societies ranged from a few members to 25 to 50 members. Most topics of discourse of these societies sound pretty weird to us today, but this was where our institutionalized science had its earliest roots.

The British Royal Society, whose full name name was The Royal Society of London for Improving Natural Knowledge, was founded in 1660. It is probably the best-known learned society in the world today, with the exception of the Swedish society that gives out the six Nobel prizes. Its publication, *Philosophical Transactions*, first published in 1665, remains one of the most prestigious scientific forums available today. The Royal Society began at a time when England was desperately trying to heal the wounds of its Reformation war which resulted in the monarch Charles I being beheaded and the Puritan government replacing the Royalist government. When Charles II was restored to the throne of England he issued his Declaration of Breda, which promised a general amnesty and freedom of conscience. Not surprisingly, he was then approached to issue a charter for and be patron of the Royal Society.

Most of the members of the Royal Society were Puritans but, as noted above, reconciliation was the order of the day. The founders included Bishop John Wilkins, a true man of science; the philosopher John Glanville; John Wallis, a mathematician; and Robert Hooke, who was a major contributor to health science with his microscope studies. When you're writing a preamble for the charter of a learned society you go to a major literary person, don't you? Well, the Royal Society got Christopher Wren instead. After the Great Fire of London he designed the new St. Paul's Cathedral and was the architect for rebuilding the city of London.

The French Académie des Sciences was established in 1666 under the patronage of—who else—Jean Baptiste Colbert. Colbert's idea was to formalize, under his own aegis, the informal, private meetings of French natural philosophers including luminaries such as René Descartes, Blaise Pascal, Pierre Gassendi and Marin Mersenne. The society first met in the royal library at Versailles. Colbert's scheme in lending his name and patronage was that he saw opportunities for investments coming from inventions generated by the leading minds of France. Colbert assumed he would be in a position to take advantage of such clever minds at work. In 1669, Colbert was pressed to reorganize the Académie and to bring in the king as patron. The society changed its name to the Académie Royale des Sciences and began issuing prizes for inventions.

One academy prize offered was for the invention of a clock that could keep accurate time on a ship at sea with a compensating apparatus that would correct for errors due to climate and weather and thus be able to calculate longitude. This was the clock invented by John Harrison, an English horologist and cabinet maker. In 1761, Harrison won a prize originally offered in 1713 by the British government for the design of a clock that measured longitude. In a test run to Jamaica, Harrison's clock was able to determine longitude to within 18 nautical miles. Harrison's clock went to theBritish navy, giving England a distinct edge over France in the Seven Years War and the Napoleonic Wars. French clockmakers, reputed to be the finest in Europe, were eclipsed by Harrison's success and the French retired their competing prize. This was another defeat for Colbert's science policy, which was a small sidebar emanating from his religious policy and his suppression of the Huguenots during the Reformation. Huguenots made up most of the French horologist trade.

Another sidebar is that in 1793, France's revolutionary government suppressed the Académie Royale des Sciences while meting out the same fate to all the other royal academies. As British industry, the British navy and the British merchant marine took over the world's mercantile leadership, some strange ways of pushing weight around began to surface. For example, the International Postal Union exempted the United Kingdom from putting the name of its country on its stamps. The special deal required that only the figure of the monarch appear on stamps. Every other country in the world was required to include the country's name.

In the beginning of the International Postal Union when everyone was concerned about the mechanics of processing mail, when every letter in the whole world was manipulated by hand and people were concerned about different languages identifying the country of origin, the British claimed that the sun never set on the British Empire, so the monarch's figure was sufficient. An exemption was made for them. That exemption has continued to the present.

That's one reward for being bloody minded enough to emerge as the winner of the Renaissance and the Reformation. Simply put, if you win that kind of a global reorganization, your whims are granted and your vote counts for more than anyone else's.

Chapter Five

Mohammed Established Islam
in a Desert

ISLAM WAS ESTABLISHED shortly after AD 600 and quickly fulfilled our generic definition of religion as a belief system designed to address the unknown and unknowable and to assist believers in living together harmoniously according to rules of conduct that address the existing social order. As a religion Islam was established to acknowledge a single god. It was founded by a merchant of Mecca named Mohammed, who claimed to have received divine revelations from that god.

Mohammed was directed in these revelations to destroy the idols in the pantheistic city of Mecca. Further, Mohammed announced that the Meccans had to acknowledge the monotheistic deity Allah and begin to worship Him exclusively. Finally, Mohammed revealed that the wealthy merchants and tribal elders would have to share their God-given wealth with the poor. This message was attractive to the poor but was less than enthusiastically received by the priests of the pantheist gods and the establishment of Mecca. In the seventh century, Mecca's establishment included a few well-to-do merchants and the chiefs and sub-chiefs of a tribal culture. This culture was a strong extended-family society based on a pervasive agricultural economy with the family heads being the local chiefs.

Mohammed's revelations were written down in what became the Qur'an, the holy book of Islam. The preserved messages are known as readings.

Mohammed attracted a few converts with a simple message. His uncle, who had raised him and taught him to be a merchant after his father had died when Mohammed was eight, and his wife, who had financed his business, both died and Mohammed was left destitute. Among the converts Mohammed attracted with his prophecies were a number from a neighbouring agricultural community named Yathrib.

In AD 622 the people of Yathrib needed a mediator to settle a number of disputes that had deteriorated into full-blown blood feuds. Mohammed enjoyed a reputation with the converts as a holy and wise man, and the people of Yathrib invited him to come to their town to exercise a quasi-judicial mediation service to adjudicate some local feuds that were wracking the community. This journey, known as the Hegira, marks the beginning of Islam.

As it emerged, Islam was a religion founded principally in law, not in a formal theology. It was established not in Mecca, but 40 miles away in the rural town of Yathrib. The name Yathrib was changed to Medina, which became known as the City of the Prophet. Medina is the second most holy site in Islam today after Mecca.

Mohammed had established a religion that was monotheistic to replace the pantheistic gods in Mecca. This religion provided a pastoral, nomadic, patriarchal and tribal people with rules to live by, which were congruent with their geographic, cultural, social and economic realities.

In AD 623, Mohammed reported a revelation in which he received permission from Allah to engage in war with the forces opposing the Islamic faith, particularly the pariah, idol-worshiping infidels who had rejected Mohammed in Mecca. It was during this period that Mohammed acquired the status of Holy Warrior. Mohammed was wounded in one of the battles but was saved by what was attributed to divine intervention. In AD 627, Mohammed broke a siege by the Meccans, and by AD 629 he had occupied Mecca, where he was acclaimed as chief and prophet. By AD 630 Mohammed had taken control of all of what we today call Saudi Arabia and the rest of the territory adjacent in the Arabian Peninsula. In seven short years, Islam had become an expansionist religion.

Mohammed's augural assumptions make Islam similar to Judaism, another religion that has its roots in a prophetic history and a legalistic founder. Unlike Judaism, Islam embraced an expansionary posture from the beginning and encouraged a basis for conversion of those adherents of other faiths. Judaism avoided any nuance of a conversionary role. The core value in Judaism is the belief that the Jews are the people chosen by God and no outsider need apply. With a similar prophetic history, Islam claims that Mohammed was dealing with revealed truth, diverging importantly from the theologically derived truth that was the mark of the Christian faith. To this day, Mohammed is referred to by Islamic faithful as the Prophet followed by the phrase "Blessings on his name."

In AD 632 Mohammed went on his last pilgrimage to Mecca. On his way back he visited Mount Arafat. It was here that he set down the protocols for this pilgrimage,

known as the hajj. It is incumbent on all devout
Muslims to engage in this pilgrimage to Mecca at least
once in their lifetime as long as they can afford it and
their pilgrimage will not cause undue hardship to their
family. After prescribing the rituals to be followed by
the faithful going on this pilgrimage, including worship-
ping at the black obelisk of the Kabba, the Prophet
became ill, went to the home of his favourite among his
nine wives and died.

Mohammed never claimed divine status for himself.
His claims were for prophetic gifts and that his prophecies were truly revealed to him by God. It was through
his prophecies that Islam justified its missionary movements to the African Atlantic coast, into Spain under
the Moorish Caliphates, to India and Indonesia.

Expansion into Eastern Europe was attempted by
the Ottoman sultans, and Charles V succeeded in holding off the Muslim incursions that reached the gates of
Vienna. Charles V, along with the Teutonic Knights and
a Polish army, turned back the Ottoman Turks but left
large pockets of Islamic faithful in parts of the Balkans
including present-day Kosovo, Albania and adjacent
parts of Greece, Macedonia and southern Russia. The
Islamic population's relations with its Christian neigh-
bours have been significant in Balkan politics to the
present day.

King Ferdinand III of Castile (then an independent
kingdom adjacent to Spain) energetically conducted a
series of wars against the Moors and defeated the
Almmohad Caliphate of Andalusia at the Battle of
Cordova. Ferdinand III conquered more Islamic land in
Spain than any other Spanish ruler and reduced the
remaining Islamic Spanish territories to the status of
vassals to the Kingdom of Castile. The Muslim pres-

ence was finally driven out of Spain at the Battle of al Hambra and the Siege of Granada in 1492 by King Ferdinand V the Catholic and Queen Isabella I of Castile, thereby completing the task of their forebear, Ferdinand III of Castile.

The Battle of Andalusia came back to the West's attention recently when Osama bin Laden, in one of his videotaped interviews from Afghanistan, spoke of the illegal removal of Islamic lands at the Battle of Andalusia in the thirteenth century. Included in Bin Laden's revisionist history was a warning that the Catholic Crusaders had killed many more Muslims during the sacking of Jerusalem and in the Andalusian campaign than Americans had died in the Twin Towers assault. The bin Laden fulmination was clearly a reference to the Qur'an's approval of blood feuds, which can extend for generations.

Mohammed's death left Islam with no designated heir. This gave rise to the period of the Caliphate (Khalifa) which was the title given to Mohammed's successors. The title applied to succeeding heads of Islamic states for the next 600 years as the institution evolved.

First there were the so-called orthodox caliphs (AD 632–661), next came the Umayyad Dynasty (AD 661–750), and as Islam became more stable, the Abbasid Dynasty followed (AD 750–1258).

Succession has always been a problem in Islam. The problem lies in the two competing tribal Islamic sects, the Sunnis and the Shi'ites. The Sunnis were a loose confederation of tribal groupings and the Shi'ites were another, smaller confederation. At contention was the control of Islam's central states.

In AD 817 Imam Reza, the eighth Shi'ite successor to the Prophet Mohammed (each sect chose its own

Caliph) was felled by poison administered by agents of the Sunni caliph Mamun while Reza was visiting the small village of Mashhad in northeastern Iran. Mashhad has since become a prosperous shrine city with two million pilgrims visiting annually. The permanent population enjoys the many benefits that accrue to those whose lot in life it is to administer a shrine complex. But things continue to get better at Iran's holiest shrine. In May 2002, Reuters news agency reported that a call centre had been installed to accommodate the congregation of those who "wanted to maintain a special relationship with His Holiness." The Reuters report went on to say that state television was showing workers at the call centre holding telephone handsets out the window so that callers might offer their prayers to the grave site.

The Shi'ites are the home base of the Wahhabis, Islam's most militant fundamentalist sect. It was the Wahhabi who provided the manpower to outfit Afghanistan's 1990s Taliban regime with clerical leadership. Wahhabi was founded in the eighteenth century in the Arabian peninsula by a holy man named Mohammed ibn Abd al-Wahhab. Since that time the Wahhabis have been busy raising money from successful souk merchants and oil lease salesmen. Members of the Wahhabi sect wielded the guns that were behind defeating the Russians in Central Asia in the late 1980s and the Saud family who traded away the oil-drilling rights in Saudi Arabia. The Wahhabis are the folks currently behind the aggressive anti-government activity in Saudi Arabia, Egypt and most other states in the Middle East.

They are hard-core in their strict fundamentalist adherance to Islam. It is the street creditability of the

Wahhabis' strict, literal approach to Muslim core beliefs that keeps governments on the edge of their cushions throughout the Middle East. The sect is an opponent of anything in the region that would even hint at liberal thought.

The Wahhabi, al Qaida and the Taliban are not the only conservative fundamentalist groups active in the Muslim world. There is the Muslim Brotherhood, which has been active in Egypt since World War I; the Islamic Salvation Front; the Armed Islamic Group, which is based in Algeria and recruits unemployed and unemployable young men. Algeria's unemployment problems were inherited from the nationalist Féderation de Libération National (FLN) who took a pass on being part of the French colonial empire and later chose not to be a part of Metropolitan France. Basically, you have to assume that wherever you go in the world that has a permanent or temporary community that includes young Muslim males, you will find a recruitment base for and a cadre of the Wahhabis.

In May 2002, Returers reported that the United Nations was having a meeting of one of its innumerable committees—the Committee on Torture—in Geneva. The chairman, Peter Thomas Burns, had invited the head of the Saudi delegation to discuss with the committee the issue of Shari'a law being used to justify beatings, amputations and torture-assisted interrogations by police agencies, and including beheadings and stonings as legal punishments. Abdulwahab A. Attar, the Saudi representative in Geneva, told the committee: "It is a question we refuse to discuss."

The Wahhabis have been much more voluble since the discovery of oil in the Middle East. Interestingly, their message has dismissed any suggestion that

Mohammed's original call for a more equitable sharing of wealth could be interpreted as a call for the oil revenues to be publicly shared in a more even-handed way. The Wahhabis take a very conservative approach to issues such as slavery, torture in police interrogations and the range of crimes meriting execution. Indeed, all of the above are the norm in the countries of the Arabian Peninsula plus many other Islamic countries.

So we see that the result of Mohammed's labours was a religious conviction providing the faithful with the assurance of life after death. To achieve this eternal life, there were certain rules to follow. The variety of the rules is pretty far-reaching, ranging from dietary laws, including the outright banning and consumption of alcohol and pork, to commercial property laws, including the treatment of slaves, a ban on collecting interest on loaned money and laws governing the complexities of life in extended families. The validity of these rules is assured by one's absolute belief that Mohammed's message was indeed a prophetic one revealed exclusively to Mohammed by God.

This message was revealed to the Prophet in the seventh century and upon his death there was no means by which the message could be amended by successors or later prophets. Changes could only come from imams and only by way of interpretation. There is in Islam no centralizing authority, only opinions holding more weight than others among Islamic scholars such as the Ulama at al-Azhar University in Cairo. The fatwa under which Salman Rushdie, author of *The Satanic Verses,* was sentenced to death, for example, could be carried out by any faithful Muslim. It was "ordered" by Ayatollah Ruhollah Khomeini, the rabhar (a religious and political leader) of Iran. No one can cancel a fatwa except the issuer. Although it can be examined for correctness by any Muslim, there is no other way to undo anything done in the name of Islam.

The message was delivered to a culture that lived in a feudal agricultural and trading society, whose rules of conduct were based on the supremacy of the patriarch (the senior male member of an extended family). Men might have four wives, as men must be prepared to marry unaccompanied female members of their extended family. These include widows, unmarried daughters of members of the family and divorced women who require protection in what was and is a volatile society. Men may divorce a wife with relative ease. Women are not permitted any grounds for divorce because to allow women rights to divorce might be construed by religious clerics as an intrusion on the functions of the entire extended family. Tunisia, however, has recently permitted women to petition for divorce.

In Islam the extended family is treated seriously as the key ingredient of the entire economy. Islam was formulated for a society living in the Middle East's harsh Arabian desert in the seventh century. The backbone of cultural values was a little bit of trade and an agriculture where the emphasis was on husbandry. In such societies worldwide, we are not surprised, historically, to find a lot of arguments and feuds. With the social and economic survival of the tribal community being vested in the extended family it is also not surprising to find that the individual's worth is suppressed beyond any point of recognition that a Westerner would easily find familiar. The concept of "blood money" is a good example of this.

If you were to have an argument with your tribal neighbour and you were to kill him, it is likely the police would arrest you as a suspect. If, after questioning, you were to confess or the police were to conclude that you had indeed killed your neighbour, a trial would be held. It would be assumed by the court that the tribe and the two families have a vested interest in the matter under dispute and the killing should not become an issue leading to a blood feud. It would be the obligation of your extended family to offer the family of the murdered man (these matters usually involve men since money and property are normally in the purview of men's responsibilities) a sum of money in payment for the loss of his life, which was the property of his extended family. Notice that the damage done is to the murdered man's extended family, not to his immediate family; the extended family has lots of experience in looking after widows and surviving children. The place where the potential for damage is greater is the tribe because if the two families extend the quarrel into a blood feud, the whole tribe will suffer economic loss. Therefore the court would be interested right off the bat in getting a blood money settlement from your family. Failing that, the court will order your execution.

There is little pretense that Islamic courts are objective or unbiased, as is expected in the West. The courts are there to settle disputes and protect the stakeholders. They are there to protect the interests of the extended family or families that make up a tribe, or the nation, but not without taking into account Islam's overriding concerns. There is certainly no concern for the individual's civil or political rights. The life of the individual is of no concern compared to the well-being of the tribe and the maintenance of the extended family's ability to deliver services to individuals. In the Islamic state there are no social services except those which are delivered through the religion. This state of affairs is fatalism in action and inshallah, the will of Allah.

In the post-9/11 days, many otherwise informed observers called for Islam to undergo a reformation, similar to the one the West had long ago undergone. To suggest that the Islamic societies undergo a reformation is akin to suggesting that they give up their religion, give up on their dispute settlement system, give up on their family structure and give up on their court system. The Islamic states are bereft of any ability to conduct any basic scientific research. If you were to visit the al-Azhar University in Cairo with the idea you were going to visit a world-class institution, you would find young men and boys sitting in lecture hall memorizing the Koran. It is being read aloud just as Western students heard the commentaries on the Bible written by long-dead Church Fathers in the medieval European scholastic universities. Just because the few Middle Eastern state-run universities turn out some graduates to do technology in some of the more obvious disciplines, is no reason to suspect that Islamic universities and Madrasses are hotbeds of research. The secrets of the universe are a topic that conservative Muslims dismiss with the catch-all phrase inshallah.

Take a look at some of the employment advertisements in the *New York Times*, the *Washington Post* or Toronto's *Globe and Mail* and see what kind of jobs are being offered by Saudi Arabia, the Emirate States and Egypt. Nurses, engineers, medical doctors, dentists and Filipino maids are required in these countries where social services consist mostly of handouts from the rulers. The compensation packages are a bit higher than the same jobs call for at home, with a solid pre-paid benefits package, home leave funding, and payment in U.S. dollars with no income tax! No income tax is an interesting issue. It means that the country's Gross National Product is so low and unemployment is so high that there is no point in taxing the population of the country. Revenues come in and are taken over by the rulers and then doled out through tribes and extended families as the rulers see fit.

Historically, Islam was one of the great learned religions. The medieval library in Alexandria was open to all and was the repository of Hellenistic and Roman thought from which the West derived its extant versions of Aristotle and, indeed, virtually the entire Greek corpus. The ancient world's understanding of the universe was collected and maintained by Islamist scholars in Alexandria until the end of the medieval period—an open and inquiring scholarship that outstripped that of the Christian world. It was the discoveries of the Renaissance and wars of conversion accompanied by a massive explosion in learning and ideation that caused the Muslim scholarship to retreat into a corrupt civil rule propped up by a rigid clericalism. This retreat was underscored by the ordinary people of Islam becoming materially poorer when they had been a wealthy civilization with diverse economic bases and strong, stable social structures.

In current global economic terms, the Islamic world is effectively sitting in the middle of the thirteenth century. Islam has not contributed to the world's mainstream of knowledge since the Middle Ages. The lesson the clerics, rulers and professionals have taken from the West is that it was a ghastly mistake to have allowed the Renaissance and Reformation to happen. Furthermore, it was an even bigger blunder to allow the

Enlightenment to occur. The idea that the individual might have some value, reaching beyond his or her own extended family, can only be seen as a high level of disregard for core Islamic beliefs.

Islam is going to have to have a reformation, but it is not going to be one that is proposed by Western commentators.

If Muslim civilizations are going to survive the next 500 years, Islam must have a reformation. There is no future for Muslims if they are to take part in a world that grows increasingly more complex and abstract and is more interactive. This reformation, if it is to be successful, must retain Islamic values that minimally allow the maintenance of the faith's traditional core of identity. We predict that to have a reformation the Muslim world must start out with reform of that all-pervasive part of Islam, the legal system known as the Shari'a.

Because of Islam's heritage as a religion without central control features and without a legalistic ordering of society, it is from Shari'a scholars that we might expect concern for a reformation to be expressed first. We would also expect that, as in the West, the first calls for a reformation would be tentative and fail to completely recognize the extent to which reform is required. Time travellers from the seventh century, who have never culturally passed through the Renaissance, will be ill-equipped to deal with the quantum, globalized, mass communications world of the third millennium.

In the fourteenth century, a major Arab historian expressed his reservations about the nature of the Islamic world. Ibn-Khaldun's thesis was that a continuing leitmotif of the Muslim world was a deep and unwavering distrust of urbanity. According to ibn-Khaldun, the itinerant and unlearned rose out of the desert intent on pressing their primordial and puritanical visions of a world view on the civilized city dwellers. With great foresight, ibn-Khaldun's concern was the frequency with which this tendency seemed to occur.

Chapter Six

Getting on with the Reformation...
Or Maybe Not

IN 1970 A Muslim scholar named Mahmoud Mohammed Taha found himself banned from participating in public events. Taha was the founder of the Sudanese Republican party, a nationalist political movement. In Sudan at the end of World War II, intellectuals, like everywhere else in Africa, were involved in nationalist politics. In Sudan, most of the political movements were under the thumb of the traditional Muslim leaders.

Taha noted that all the nationalist parties were failing to address what he saw as the real issues. The Republican party recognized that political change was unlikely without a reformation occurring coincidentally in Islam. The party had little political success and Taha began to push the idea, among the disciples he had gathered around him, that it was urgent to begin the process of complete reform of Islam. Over the next twenty years Taha managed to write a complete system that set out an all-inclusive method to reinterpret the whole of Islam. This work he published under the title *The Second Message of Islam*, a book which in the words of one of his followers, Abdulla Ahmed An-Na'im, constituted "a modern and revolutionary interpretation of the Qur'an." Given Islamic reluctance about updating

Mohammed's revelations that had resulted in the Qur'an, the book was bound to attract attention.

The government of Sudan was headed by a warlord named Numayry. Numayry was the leader of a group of young officers who had taken over the country. The problem was that Sudan had (and has) two parts: a Muslim north and a non-Muslim south. Numayry reached an accommodation with the Muslim leadership of the north. Under their influence he began to take a conservative interpretation of the Qur'an and enforce compliance of the fundamentalist stand on Islamic law.

Taha and his band of followers had already managed to come to the attention of the government security forces and suffered the usual harassments and restrictions on meetings from the government. When Taha made a call for resistance to Numayry's campaign to force the south to accept Qur'anic compliance, Taha and his Republicans were jailed without any charges being laid. After a year and a half in jail, the Republicans were released. Then Taha was rearrested, charged with sedition and various catch-all offenses. He was executed on market day in Khartoum's town square.

Abdulla Ahmed An-Na'im, a law professor who had become a member of Taha's Republicans, managed to negotiate releases for nearly 400 of the Republicans with the understanding that the political party would be discontinued and the organization would be formally closed down. An-Na'im became Taha's de facto successor, trying to produce the outline of an Islamic reformation which would satisfy the traditionalists as well as those who insisted that the only way was to abandon the traditional belief structure and go all out with a secular system, as the West had done. Since the early 1970s, the Republican Brotherhood followers of Taha have been spreading his ideas for the reform of Islam under the informal leadership of An-Na'im, who has been lecturing and teaching outside of Sudan.

An-Na'im has published a translation of *The Second Message of Islam* into English. He has also written a book, published by Syracuse University Press, called *Toward an Islamic Reformation: Civil Rights, Human Rights and International Law*. He has also authored *Sudanese Criminal Law*. It becomes clear why An-Na'im has been teaching at Emory University after a tour at the Woodrow Wilson International Center for Scholars in Washington, D.C. and a year at the University of Saskatchewan, where he held a chair in Human Rights: none of these institutions are close to any centres of Islamic teaching or assassination.

Anyone who wants to ask difficult questions should raise the issue that Islamic law is missing a critical subiscipline that is essential to a legal system in the third millennium. This sub-discipline is one that neither the North American free trade zone, nor the European Union nor Russia can get along without: administrative law. Administrative law is the glue that holds together the complex rules of the World Trade Organization and national, state or provincial laws that feed into the global rules governing trade, labour practices, intellectual property rules, the harmonization standards by which manufacturing standards are the same for trading partners, and the regulations for border clearing and international transportation co-operation.

Administrative laws are the fiats that a civil servant looks up in the European Union which allows the citizens of one European country to go to another country to work without hindrance. Administrative law permits the European Union to produce a new currency to be adopted by all, with a few notable exceptions, and those exceptions are required to allow the euro to circulate freely and, of course, to buy stuff.

Islamic law, concerned as it is with regulation of the extended family, is absolutely indifferent to making allowance, as an example, for a Mexican truck coming from Mexico with fresh vegetables being able to pass highway safety standards in the United States and Canada. Islam has never had need for administrative law. As long as the extended family is controlled and is held accountable for its members, Islamic law has no need to train clerics, who are legally inclined, to adjudicate disputes that are either in the province of an absolute ruler or the problem of the head of an extended family. You don't really need a broad legal philosophy governing highways when, historically, all your extraterritorial travel involves a camel caravan and the camel master's honesty.

The West has been very emphatic in its claims of not having any objection to Islam as a religion. It has emphasized that it is only interested in the terrorists and those who feed, house and supply them. In the post 9/11 period, Muslim spokesmen have expressed their doubts about the sincerity of the West in making this claim to hold a benign view of Islamic religion.

Muslims have spoken regularly about the United States' use of Israel as a surrogate in return for Israel's being granted autonomous territorial claims in what is Arab land in Palestine. It should be noted that what is at stake here is the definition of land, property and ownership, and what legal system is used to articulate the issue of land ownership. Is the legal system being asked to adjudicate whether the land is legally occupied by a tribal society made up of extended families or whether, in 1948, the United Nations could redeem an old League of Nations trusteeship mandated to Great Britain and grant the property instead to Israel?

If you are an ordinary person in an Islamic country you might be forgiven if you don't believe the Western leaders or other spokespersons. You know that the West does not respect women, and children do not respect their parents. You also feel a little bit sorry for them. It must be awful not to live within the confines of an extended family. Everyone knows that Westerners have no comparable contact that occurs in a true extended family, and that Westerners have no legally binding set of obligations and counter-obligations with their many cousins. Indeed you have heard that in the West there is very little an extended family is obligated to do for its members. There are not even rules set down about what percentage of a patrimony every good man must leave to his sons with religious sanctions to back it up. To the ordinary Muslim, unless the extend-ed family works, there will obviously be chaos.

There is the case where influential Westerners have argued that Muslims constitute a very present danger to the West. In his book *The Clash of Civilizations and the Remaking of the New World Order*, Samuel P. Huntington paints a gloomy picture of the probable outcome of Islam's assumption that conflict with the West is inevitable. Huntington is truly a distinguished student of Islam and is Alfred J. Weatherhead III Professor at Harvard University. He is also the director of Harvard's John M. Olin Institute for Strategic Studies. More importantly, he was the director of security planning for the National Security Council during the Carter admin-istration. He consults regularly in Washington, D.C. on Middle Eastern affairs. In *The Clash of Civilizations*

Huntington argues that

> Islam is a source of instability in the world because it
> lacks a dominant center. States aspiring to be leaders
> of Islam, such as Saudi Arabia, Iran, Pakistan, Turkey
> and potentially Indonesia, compete for influence in
> the Muslim world, no one of them is in a strong posi-
> tion to mediate conflicts within Islam; and no one of
> them is in a position to act authoritatively on behalf
> of Islam in dealing with conflicts between Muslim
> and non-Muslim groups. Finally, and most important,
> the demographic explosion in Muslim societies and
> the availability of large numbers of often unem-
> ployed males between the ages of fifteen and thirty is
> a natural source of instability and violence both with
> in Islam and against non-Muslims. Whatever causes
> may have been at work, this factor alone is enough
> and would go a long way to explaining Muslim vio-
> lence in the 1980s and 1990s.

Huntington is deeply concerned by a heightened
birth rate in Islamic countries, particularly in Central
Asia. He sees this birth rate as having a potential to
cause a full-blown war with the West. As noted above,
Huntington is an establishment academic and public
service figure well known in the corridors of
Washington, D.C. and New York power. That he holds
such a bleak, foreboding view of the future of Islamic
and Western relations is instructive. It has even caused
him to rethink some traditional political science terms.
The title of his seminal work, *The Clash of Civilizations*,
would have been called *The Clash of Nations* if
Huntington had written it a generation before. There is
no way to think of any Islamic nation threatening the

West, but if you feel that Islam is a threat, then you must recognize that the threat comes not from a single nation or group of nations but from the entire civilization of Islamic influence. The idea is that the globe is now pluralistic enough and its diversity is sufficiently expansive to afford it to have multiple civilizations.

The switch from "nations" to "civilizations" is also familar to readers of Bernard Lewis, Emeritus Professor of Near East Studies at Princeton University. Before going to Princeton he was Professor of The History of The Middle East at the School of Oriental and African Studies at the University of London. Lewis is to some eyes, controversial. His book *The Middle East*, published by Phoenix, covers 2,000 years of the history of the Middle East. It is encouraging to find a great scholar by global standards who does his own translations from Arabic and Persian, simply because he is the most rigorous translator he knows. What makes him controversial is his public support of the Turkish side of the claim that the Turks engaged in an Armenian genocide in World War I.

Muslims believe they are born into the family of Islam where there are a set of rules agreed on by all other Muslims and are codified in the Qur'an. The details may differ from community to community but the reasons for the rules are clearly set out. Muslims live in a world that is governed by an all-encompassing social contract of rules set down in early medieval times. To break these rules is a breech of not just the social contract but of an eternal contract with Allah. The legal system is totally congruent with the religion, controlling every facet of life, beginning with the family unit and all the intimacies involved therein.

All commercial and social life is equally controlled.

This society places no value on education except for a clerical or legal education, which is transmitted using the same pedagogy that was in vogue in the West during the scholastic period of the Middle Ages. Literacy for children consists of schooling to a grade four or eight level for most of the population; this primitive level of education also applies to those in urban settings. In the smaller urban centres education may be extended for men but there is no benefit to the extended family in educating women. Since the Muslim world is estimated to be about 90 percent rural, there is no benefit in educating boys, especially when the family needs boys to be economically productive from an early age. The exception to this pattern of education is that of young males from the minuscule upper class. They are usually educated overseas.

Demographic data incorporates education, which includes apprenticeships. Usually a male child in a village or a town will be apprenticed to a neighbour, let us say a blacksmith. After about five years, voila!, we have a new, qualified blacksmith. We know that the new blacksmith is qualified because if we live in the community, we saw him at 11 or 12 years of age beginning his career pumping the handheld bellows to get the open hearth furnace to the desired temperature. We also saw him preparing charcoal a year or so earlier, while he was getting to know the job and seeing if he and the blacksmith would get along. Another two or three years after that we saw him making crude metal items, and by the time he was 15 or so he was assisting the blacksmith in repairing farm implements. By the time he was 18 the blacksmith was thinking about retirement or the boy was thinking about finding a community that wanted a blacksmith and that his extended family would help him settle into. This is not a community that readily recognizes the need for a post-secondary community college system. This society is also not one that institutionalizes "Take your daughter to work day."

This is not a society where there is a mass outpouring of popular enthusiasm for a globally recognizable system of administrative law. Abdulla Ahmed An-Na'im addresses this point when he remarks that the majority of Muslim nation states had approached some degree of public law reform after the nineteenth century. Only family law and inheritance law relating to bequests for Muslims were left to the jurisdiction of the Shari'a.

In Islamic law there is a legal theory that says the ruler has the right to define and confine the jurisdiction of his courts. An-Na'im points out that this was a procedural shortcut which permitted the ruler to confine the application of Shari'a to matters of personal law for Muslims. The example given by An-Na'im is that in 1931 the Egyptian courts, in a move to inhibit child marriages, barred matrimonial relief in the courts in cases where the husband had not reached the age of 18 and the wife was required to be 16.

Another rule was enacted in Sudan. It allowed for the selection of any opinion within a specific school of Islamic jurisprudence, and not necessarily the dominant opinion within the given school. This was a stratagem adopted to allow courts to cut and paste opinions from one or more schools of Islamic legal points of view. It was done to allow new Sunni thought to be accessed by a jurist hearing personal law cases.

In 1956, Tunisian law found itself involved in matters of divorce and polygamy. The Tunisian court ruled that no husband could secure a divorce and no divorce would be granted unless the court consented. It further required the husband to pay a court-agreed sum, if, in the court's opinion, the husband had insufficient reasons for divorcing his wife or had caused her hardship by divorcing her. In Syria and Iraq an attempt was made to modify provisions of the laws governing polygamous marriages to require that the court obtain evidence of consent and withhold its agreement if it was unsatisfied that the consent from co-wives had been secured.

There is one case where An-Na'im feels that the attempts at reform were too radical. Tunisian marriage law was rewritten to outlaw polygamy altogether on the grounds that the satisfaction of the Qur'anic laws on polygamy assuring justice for all co-wives was, as a practical matter, impossible for any man excepting the Prophet.

Another Qur'anic rubric says that a ruler may implement administrative decisions that are advantageous and not inimical to Shari'a. The example that An-Na'im gives is interesting. An action is brought to require a wife to obey her husband. No problem there: Shari'a requires a wife to obey. But what happens when the couple has children? If a wife became disobedient and the children were over five years old, the court could, at its discretion, place the children with whichever parent it deemed would serve the interests of justice best, with full regard for the welfare of the children. If the children are under five they stay with the mother.

Chapter Seven

Islam and Civil Liberties

THE ISLAMIC CIVILIZATION has had a rough time since the thirteenth century. Not only was Islamic outward expansion ground to a halt but Islam's warriors were then driven out of Europe and defeated in crucial battles in Andalusia and at the portal of Europe proper, the gates of Vienna. The worst cosmic case scenario was yet to come. Islam was about to meet Western imperialism on the march. By the twentieth century the Islamic world would come out a poor second—known only for its natural resource supplies.

It is *de rigeur* for Islamic leaders and journalists to blame the West for their poverty and the lifestyle-limiting options available to them. Saying this is not a defense of Western imperialism. The truth is that there have been an amazing collection of corrupt Muslim leaders since the fourteenth century. To claim, as more that one Muslim leader has, that Western civil liberties are an invitation to revolt and that open society would be destructive to the revealed truth of Islam, invariably lays the claimant open to charges of selective reading of history. The truth is that Islam's legal system was barred from developing administrative systems because to do so would intrude on the prerogatives of the extended family. So while the West was learning how to create a legal system to manage an expanding economy, Islam kept to its souks and to animal husbandry, operating as if the globe were populated by a series of small feudal villages or fiefdoms. Islamic extraterritorial trading was opportunistic without administrative procedures to stabilize growth.

Administrative law began in the West with the Reformation. Sir Edward Coke, Lord Chief Justice of England, needed to distance himself from canon law when in 1628 he ruled in the Sutton's Hospital case that "they [corporations] cannot commit treason, nor be outlawed, nor excommunicate for they have no souls." Coke had, in this one simple ruling, banned the bishops' courts from exercising canonical authority over civil matters. There is no way to do this with Shari'a. Western commentators have pointed a finger of scorn at Islam every time one of its leaders launched a grandiose reformist plan or tried to graft Islamic terms of reference onto Western ideologies such as communism and socialism. Leaders such as Gamel Abdel Nasser, the late President of Egypt; Ayatolla Khomeini, the cleric-leader of the Iranian revolution; Saddam Hussein, President of Iraq; Mu'ammer Gaddafi, with his Islamization Project in Libya via the Green Book; and Osama bin Laden are among the more prominent examples of leaders who possessed impeccable Muslim credentials and tried to challenge the usefulness of the Western open society.

The means by which the West has rejected the closed, or from an Islamic point of view, all-encompassing worldview, has been to trivialize Muslim values. In Muslim eyes, the West not only trivializes Islam, but by assuming that one belief system is of equal value compared to another, trivializes the validity of the prophetic voice of Mohammed. The most frequent critique of the West by Muslim thinkers is that the West's social openness is a tool in Satan's hand. And in Islam, Satan is a potent figure. To a Muslim the personage of Satan is not merely the leader of a band of renegade cast-out angels; Satan is the great tempter. Satan tempts the ill-informed or the should-know-betters with such deliciously seductive offers that they will have no choice but to adopt the infidel's lifestyle and be dammed for eternity.

To the devout Muslim, it is only by the state and the clergy employing Qur'anically-guided bans on designated thoughts and actions that the great mass of the population will be protected from Satan's temptations. To an Islamic leader, the choice is simple.

Take for example freedom of speech. Rather than being faced with an untold number of people being led into sin by a writer, broadcaster, poet, journalist, editor, publisher or the author of tempting ideas, it becomes necessary by all means to stop distribution of the offending material. A good example of this is the fatwa that was issued by Ayatolla Khomeini in 1988 against Salman Rushdie for his book *The Satanic Verses*. The edict authorized any Muslim to kill Rushdie, even in violation of the laws of the country of Rushdie's citizenship, the United Kingdom. Rushdie was raised a Muslim and was nominally a Muslim, and that was enough for Khomeini. In fact, one film producer in Pakistan made a movie, which enjoyed great popularity in the Islamic world, showing a band of Islamic commandos engaging in a derring-do raid to overcome Rushdie's guards and carry out the fatwa. Even in relatively moderate Islamic states such as Egypt, when the Nobel Laureate Naguib Mahfouz was stabbed and nearly killed, an Interior Ministry spokesman commented that the writer should not offend pious Muslims with his non-Islamic writings and would have been better off had he moved to the West where such writing was tolerated. In any event, the perpetrator has not been apprehended.

The idea of an open society is relatively recent. It was probably John Locke who started the ball rolling. The ball rolled to the United States where it developed into a cultural hallmark. The truth is that an open society is, as far as we can tell, the most effective means of harnessing the creative resources of the entire culture. Whether this process ultimately serves the interests of the society's establishment rather than its poor is a question that is greatly contested.

The inevitability of openness is pretty clear. For example, Islam originally enforced a strict form of the Shari'a state where the law did not apply to non-Muslims. Where Islam had conquered territories, as in Spain for example, this was found to be inadequate. Islamic jurisprudence then moved to a position in which Shari'a became the general law, applicable to everyone, with exceptions being made only in very special cases. This situation was similar to the requirement, up until recently, to have a day of rest, a sabbath day, a holy day or the Lord's day in North America—always on Sunday. After the period of the great religious revival in the 1870s, legislation was passed in numerous states, provinces and municipalities which required observance of one of these days of religious non-activity. No work was to be done. Then the exclusions started. First "essential" services were defined. Hospitals were exempt, but only by name, for fear someone would claim to be a hospital. Drugstores were allowed to open, but only for the purpose of selling medical supplies. Then some marginal Christian congregations, who followed the Jewish tradition of sundown Friday until sundown Saturday, were exempted. Next, special dispensation was made for allowing organized sports (but not professional sports) to be played on Sunday. Then Jews were allowed to open places of business on Sunday as long as they closed down on Saturday.

Islam moved away from strict Shari'a whenever it had a majority of the population and then quickly moved into granting dispensations from specific requirements. For example, the Qur'an states that slaves must be prisoners of war. But what if a slave trader were to offer you slaves who were already slaves? The clerics who were the Shari'a judges ruled that Islam had rules to cover treatment of slaves and therefore it was all right to acquire slaves who were not prisoners of war. These slaves just happened to be Nubians (black Africans). The die was cast and Arabia became the centre of the slaving business. Being in the slavery business led to even more corruption in Arabia and Africa.

The forward-thinking Islamists who have attempted to prove that a reformation is possible without losing Islam's central goals have not been keeping up with that influential body of thinkers, the Ulama at al-Azhar University in Cairo. After prayerful study the Ulama prepared a draft Islamic constitution in 1978. This draft somehow failed to mention the rights and entitlements of non-Muslim citizens in the notional Islamic country the Ulama wished to create. The document also failed to account for the disposition of any residual slaves who would be left over from a predecessor state or who would be passing through with their masters. Finally, this document, created by the leading minds of Islam, did not reveal whether non-Muslims would qualify as citizens in this notional Islamic state.

The definition of citizenship is one of the monster problems for constitutionalists everywhere in the world because there is a lot of movement in the world: emigration, immigration, countries being overrun and refugees overrunning, economic refugees, children sponsoring their parents as immigrants. The question of citizenship looms larger and larger as the dispossessed become desperate for a place that will grant them the "right" to stay there.

The principal economic unit in the Islamic world is the extended family. In the West we are accustomed to centrality being imposed by government. With a Muslim theocratic government there is no central authority. The institution of political power is the tribe or extended family and this power base is not about to have its ability to provide care for its members—which in the West would come from government—diminished in any way. There is no welfare in Islamic countries; subsistence grants come from the family. Westerners have asked how the unemployed young men who make up the Islamic terrorists groups manage to live in Algeria. The answer is that they are supported by their extended families and usually find minor criminal activity a way to make up the shortfall from the family's small offerings. The result is that it would never occur to the government of Algeria to intrude on the prerogatives of the extended families and institute a welfare program, especially in a country where the fifteen-to-thirty-five-year-old age group has a fifty percent unemployment rate.

Of course another problem in Algeria is that the Algerian army has two armed domestic enemies to face.

There is the Armed Islamic Group (GIA) who are Islamic fundamentalistsdedicated to a revolutionary movement. The GIA accuses the FLN, who originally deposed the French colonial rulers after World War II, of having the nationalist revolution and then failing to make the move to an Islamic state. Obviously, the FLN is not pure enough in its practice of Islam. The fundamentalists actually won the last election in Algeria, but the army staged a coup. The Algerian army receives military aid from the United States and France, and is a strong supporter of a secular state, especially of a secular army.

The other armed enemy the Algerian government and military are facing is the nomadic Berber tribes. The Berbers claim they are the original tribal inhabitants of the land that is now Algeria and that they have been driven from their ancestral lands. They too are in armed rebellion. Just to make things more complicated, the Berbers are also at war with the fundamentalists. In case you don't recognize the Berbers, think back to those French Foreign Legion movies on the late, late show made before 1939. The Berbers were who the French were fighting. Simply put, the Berber position is that they want the usurpers off their ancestral lands, which is their right, according to the Qur'an. Since the idea of an Islamic state is a relatively recent one, and pastoral grazing rights are pretty clearly guaranteed in the Qur'an, you don't have to be a Muslim cleric specializing in property law to figure this one out. All of this makes Algeria a classic three-way bind. The Shari'a requires that the disputants settle the grazing rights first. After all, the original Arabian peninsula was pretty sparse land and North Africa is no better. If you allow politics to decide the priorities of these things, all of the camels, sheep and goats will have died before you have a meeting arranged between the Berbers, the GIA and the Algerian army.

Civil rights are a non-issue in Islam where the only rights a person has are defined by the extended family and tribal custom. For example, in a world where banditry is relatively common, the Koran is clear on how you must treat a strange visitor, even to the point of defining the moment when a visitor becomes a guest instead of a stranger. That moment is when you offer the stranger a cup of tea and the stranger accepts the cup of tea. When you have induced the stranger to accept your hospitality, at that point you are absolutely committed to doing no harm to the now guest, and the guest, by accepting your hospitality, is absolutely committed to doing you no harm.

This hospitality sharing is a custom that extends all over the Muslim world. There are numerous examples of knowledgeable travellers in the Muslim world being in tense meetings and impatiently waiting for the tea to be served because they had complete faith in the unlikelihood of their host's breaching the Koranic injunction against injuring someone whom they had converted to guest status. It's a nice civility code in a very poor part of the world. It holds from the poorest peasant to the wealthiest sheik and is a universal mark of generosity throughout Islam. That such institutionalizing of a basic social code was necessary enough for Mohammed to include in the Koran gives you an idea of what the traveller could expect as the norm unless the tea was forthcoming.

Commenting on the Ulama methods of discourse and disputation, Farish A. Noor is disturbed that in an era of globalization, where more and more Muslims find

themselves living in Islamically non-homogenious societies, the Ulama have allowed an "unnatural halt to the
process of intellectual debate and contestation." He
sees that "the internal dynamics of the Shari'a have
been lost."

Throughout his book on reforming Islamic law,
Abdulla An-Na'im frequently reminds us that central to
the understanding of how Islam differs from other
world religions is the "universality and centrality of religion as a factor in the lives of the Muslim people."
While this is undoubtedly true, it appears that
Westerners must also appreciate that the exploitation
and enhancement of the role of the extended family is
probably the point we need to focus on if we want to
understand the limits of our acceptance in the Muslim
world.

The Prophet was not merely being opportunistic in
selecting the extended family as the key point of access
to the population and the economy in establishing a
theocratic legal system. The extended family was
already established as the key to the tribal structure of
the region. The rapid expansion of Islam, after the
Prophet's death, proved how right he was to use this
strategy.

In 1981 Bernard Lewis wrote a prescient chapter
entitled "The Return of Islam" in a book edited by
Michael Curtis, *Religion and Politics in the Middle East*.
Lewis states that "Islam, from the lifetime of its
founder, was the state, and the identity of religion and
government is indelibly stamped on the memory and
awareness of the faithful from their own sacred writings, history and experience." It is this total identifica-
tion with Islam by the great mass of faithful Muslims
that creates the unity of Islamic purpose. One charac-

teristic that stands out among Muslims is a strong sense of honour.

If you choose to impugn the honour of a Muslim, you can forget about getting any tea from him. You have just made an enemy for life, and you can add all the members of his extended family. In the post 9/11 period, the American commentators on all the cable news channels were agonizingly asking, "Why do the Muslims hate us enough to hit the World Trade Center with hi-jacked planes?" The reason the Muslims don't like the West is quite simple. People, political leaders, intellectuals, religious leaders and the military don't take Islam seriously, and that is an insult to a Muslim's sense of self-respect and honour. The things the Muslims take seriously, the West doesn't take at all seriously. By showing its disrespect for Muslim cultural values, the Western world shows its disrespect of all Islam. For the Westerner, it is a little difficult to respect a society that is content to live in the seventh century, when by looking out the window one can see that it is, in fact, the twenty-first century.

In the West, Islamic honour looks a lot like macho pride. The difference is that this pride is being held by someone who is very sensitive about being from a culture that can't offer any of the popular cultural artifacts that, from the viewpoint of his television screen, are available to everyone who lives in the West.

There is another important factor that is part of Islamic civilization. When Muslims are in the minority of the population they tend to be very vocal about their complaints with the society's rules, whenever they favor the majority. Their complaints tend to be related to the rules making it, as they say, difficult to be a practicing Muslim. When they are in the majority, however,

Muslims pass laws transferring the legal system to a Shari'a basis. This has recently happened in Nigeria where the northern provinces have become Shari'a legal enclaves and two women have been sentenced to be stoned to death—one after being raped (which was defined by the courts as adultery) and one for bearing a child out of wedlock. Recent events in Turkey demonstrate that the previously secular Islamic state may also be on the road to becoming a fundamentalist Islamic state. In June of 2002, the religious party which is the official opposition, was awarded the Education portfolio in a cabinet reorganization. To have a new government in Turkey, led by the religious party, would have people rethinking Turkey as a member of NATO and a candidate for European Union membership.

There are a number of quite respectable ways to organize a society other than as a democracy or a federal republic. When the government is an Islamic state, like Pakistan or Saudi Arabia or a few dozen more countries across the world, the idea of civil liberties for the individual or a lack of autocracy in the ruler doesn't come up very often. Shari'a, in the eyes of a Westerner, appears somewhat on the harsh side: the police use torture and tend to get a lot of confessions. In Turkey, a secular and principally Muslim state, the main opposition is a clerical opposition, intent on establishing an Islamic state. Turkey avoids this possibility by having a constitution banning a religious state and by providing each new generation with only secular schools to attend. As noted above, however, constitutions can be changed.

You're not going to find much support among Muslims for the West's objections to the way Islam treats women, the lack of respect Islam shows towards civil liberties and the cultural spin-offs the Muslims derive from fatalism and destiny. Fatalism and destiny cause the divide between the civilization of the West and the Islamic civilization to become wider and wider the more the two civilizations interface with one another. Muslims don't understand Western family mores and frequently wonder if Westerners love their children because they spend so little time with them.

Chapter Eight

Human Rights for Muslims

THE IDEA OF human rights is a relatively recent invention in human history. Looking over this history, human rights doesn't seem to have been high on the evolutionary priority scale. It was a long time gestating. The short period that mankind has lived with such basic human rights as freedom from slavery, freedom from gender discrimination, and the right not to be legally bound to a piece of land, has arrived relatively recently, and these freedoms are still unavailable in many parts of the globe.

The human rights institutional agenda in the West has only been initiated in the past fifty years or so. In the Islamic civilization the concern for human rights has been on the level of putting the best face possible on slavery, when, as when for example, the Anti-Slavery Society of London exposed some Sudanese sheikdom in 2000 for keeping, selling slaves or punishing escaping slaves by execution or mutilation.

Unsurprisingly, it is with the issue of human rights that the Islamic reformationists have the biggest problem. In his book *Toward an Islamic Reformation*, Abdulla An-Na'im waits until the concluding chapter, as if he were aware that human rights was going to be the last pillar of Muslim wisdom that would fall before before an Islamic reformation could be negotiated. The only problem is that if An-Na'im doesn't solve this problem, he will never, in the real world, get to the relatively soft, squishy problems he has dealt with in the preceding six chapters, like administrative law. If his goal is to catch up, economically and educationally, with the rest of the world, Islam as a legal system has to be prepared to offer specific human rights to each individual. Rights cannot be subcontracted from a distant but all-pervasive extended family, or from a tribal entity beyond the family.

In the third paragraph of the chapter on human rights, An-Na'im puts on the grimace of a constitutional lawyer facing up to the problem. He has, in an earlier paragraph, while discussing the Universal Standards of Human Rights Charter adopted by the United Nations said, "If they implement Shari'a, Muslims cannot exercise their right to self-determination without violating the rights of others." He goes on to ask: "Why should universal human rights be a criterion for judging Shari'a and an objective of modern Islamic public law?"

Well for one thing, article 1.3 of the UN Charter imposes, as a condition of membership on all member nations, the agreement to cooperate in promoting and encouraging respect for human rights and fundamental freedoms for all, without distinction as to race, sex or religion. This article was adopted by the UN in 1948 and is binding on all members. The few nations which are not members of the UN are nevertheless bound by the substance of those principles of customary international law codified by the Charter.

An-Na'im then proceeds to argue that because no one has ever operationally defined the meaning of "human rights," the golden rule of doing unto others as you would have them treat you should be good enough. He neglects to mention that the UN war crimes court in The Hague is in the business of operationally defining human rights—and that it's going to be a Western definition. Assuming you're not worried about war crimes, An-Na'im notes that to carry out the golden rule you have to establish a rule of reciprocity. He points out that historically, Shari'a has treated women and non-Muslims in a non-reciprocal way, but he doesn't raise the topic of slaves, whether prisoners of war or not.

After some unconvincing arguments, An-Na'im says that universal human rights can be described in very basic terms. He says that it is part of the universal human condition to be motivated by the wish to live and to want to be free. He says all other universal human rights come from extrapolation of this will to live and to desire freedom. The desire to live brings about a desire for food and shelter and to be free from physical constraints. It is also the driving force behind the pursuit of spiritual, moral and artistic well-being.

Tell that one to Naguib Mahfouz, whom we mentioned in Chapter Seven, the Islamic world's only Nobel Laureate for Literature who was stabbed in Cairo because he offended some individual. Tell it to Salman Rushdie, who has spent years of his life having to be protected by the Special Air Service (SAS) with all the inconveniences and dangers that entails.

However, remember that the Muslim description of Satan is the great tempter. Satan puts a Muslim's soul at risk through temptation. Satan is not unabashed evil— the evil lies in man because man gives into, or is seduced by, temptation. It is good not to give into temptation, but it is safer to identify temptations, whatever their form, and destroy the creator of the temptation. Satan unleashes temptations, and the temptations seduce man to sin and to enjoy sin. It is up to the servants of Islam to outlaw temptations through the Shari'a and therefore not to allow believers to risk being tempted. In Afghanistan the literalists of the Taliban movement took the fear of the Tempter to new highs. The Taliban set themselves up as the protagonists to Satan and placed the whole of Afghanistan under an interdiction to the forces of temptation. But Afghanistan is not the only part of Islamic civilization to see the Tempter as the great enemy. If Islam has a claim to universality, it is in this view of Satan.

On April 22, 2002, Thomas Axworthy, former Principal Secretary to Pierre Elliot Trudeau, the long-serving Canadian Prime Minister, delivered a paper at the John F. Kennedy School of Government at Harvard University. The title of the paper was "Doing Evil to Do Good." Of interest to us here were his comments on the Treaty of Westphalia, which ended the Thirty Years War in 1648. He reminds us that the treaty was a break-through

> not only for ending the Thirty Years War but for con-structing an international system with some sem-blance of order. The Protestant Reformation had split the universal Catholic Church, and in that age of religious zealots war was conducted in the name of religion. Entire populations were obliged to change their faiths on the basis of whatever army triumphed on the battlefield... All signatories confirmed the facts on the ground, i.e., whoever rules determines the religion of his subjects. It was a partition principle. But Westphalia also declared that no country had

a right to intervene in the process. Rulers of one faith were to refrain from inciting uprisings of their co-religionists. With religion removed as an excuse for war, non-interference became one of the critical elements regulating the conduct of states. Non-interference, the *bete noire* of human rights activists of today, was the human rights solution to the seventeenth century religious wars that had reduced the population of central Europe by a third—more than the Black Death. By putting the lid on religious extremists, Westphalia allowed time for the virtue of pluralism to grow. In 1667, John Locke published his *Essay on Toleration* and by the eighteenth century, the age of Enlightenment made the religious frenzy of the previous century look like an aberration. The non-interference principle had worked.

Having made the case for the non-interference principle of Westphalia, Axworthy then reminded his audience that the caveat against interference had resulted in some grotesque results in the twentieth century. He pointed to the murder in 1994 of 800,000 Rwandan Tutus by the Rwandan Hutus. Mostly the murders were committed with intensely personal weapons such as knives and machetes. The UN Security Council invoked a Westphalian solution in Rwanda, despite the repeated requests of General Romeo Dallaire, head of the UN peacekeeping mission, for more troops and authority to engage the mobs of killers.

By and large the Western world has now come to accept interference, as in Kosovo, where the West came to the support of a Muslim minority and NATO forces intervened against the Serbian army. It is notable that in the case of Kosovo, the Islamic world was unwilling to assist its co-religionists. The leading paper in the Middle East, *Al-Ahram*, commented that Islam had not developed the cultural infrastructure necessary to enable Muslim countries to assist Muslim states under attack directly, to assist NATO militarily, or to assist the Red Crescent Society in humanitarian efforts. The burden of the Kosavar mission and the later mission in Bosnia fell on the West.

The issue of human rights is not one that Islamic countries feel comfortable with. Human rights fall within the purview of the extended family and there is little incentive for a Muslim nation-state to even begin to nibble away at the human rights Pandora's box. Any Islamic government policy advisor knows that if you start to put human rights into play, unless you do it in a way that completely covers it with a blanket of Shari'a justification, you will run head-on into the extended family. No matter what any Islamic legal reformist tells you, there is no way you can negotiate away the extended family.

Muslims continue to live under a legal system meant for a rural people who depend on extended family-size units for social and economic management and to provide an extended sense of collective identity. Islam does not have a theological side for it to readily amend its doctrine or dogma. Islam is a revealed religion, revealed only to the Prophet, Mohammed, without a central authority. Any moves in Islam to allow for human rights to extend to the individual are on a road covered with crater-size potholes. There is no cultural history in Islam that gives any reformer space to negotiate. Across the length and breadth of Islam—from the Atlantic coast of Africa, along the Mediterranean coast, into the Indian Ocean, and along to India and Indonesia—wher-

ever Muslims extended their faith, they took with them
a social order that worked for people who were poor
and who were able to adjust to a social order based on
the extended family and a tribal sensibility of cohesive-
ness. The Western idea of individual primacy implies
isolation and a lack of a social safe' y net. Who will be
there if one trips on any of the vicissitudes that occur in
a lifetime?

There is a word that occurs with some frequency
when you read Islamic writings, whether the writings
are commentaries on Shari'a, or devastating critiques by
a member of the Ulama or little inspirational messages
in *Al-Ahram*. That word is Sunna and it refers to model
behavior as cited by Mohammed in the Qur'an. It also
refers to the justification for Shari'a where the law is
drawn from one of the Sunna examples of model behav-
iour.

Chapter Nine

International Law and Islam

ISLAMIC COUNTRIES DO not have much trouble with international law; they don't encourage much in the way of international interference. As we saw, when the United Nations questioned the use of Shari'a to justify beatings, amputations, stonings and beheadings during a meeting of its Committee on Torture, the Saudia Arabian representative to the United Nations in Geneva stated: "It is a question we refuse to discuss."

The privacy of the extended family, with its distancing of the external world, provides little opportunity for the Islamist to address distant foreign governments as organizations to be treated with respect, if not deference. Trade relations are matters beyond significance to the average Muslim and better left to a ruler or state.

War is still organized with a tribal sensibility and tribal allegiances. For the Islamist, the idea of a Muslim army allying itself with someone beyond the level of a tribal relationship is a little bizarre. The West has learned this recently in Afghanistan where warlords and tribal leaders made side-deals with the "enemy" to allow prisoners to escape and made a show of independent action or non-action. If the warlord had not finished negotiating payment, there was no one above him who could speak for any tribal chief. In other words, effective organization beyond the extended family and the tribe is not a given in any Islamic force. If you want to know why the Israeli Army, drawing on a population base of only three million, has managed to defeat Arab armies drawn from populations of many millions, imagine the problems of organization facing the Arab commanders. If your largest force is tribal in structure you are talking about 500 to 1,500 men who have no experience in giving their loyalty to anyone higher than their unit commander. Imagine the corruption that exists in all Arab armies as supplies fall from the army trucks into the waiting arms of someone's cousin. Also, imagine the trepidation of a Western general who is ordered to integrate an Arab force within his force's disciplined ranks. And imagine the ordinary Muslim soldier in Afghanistan whose distrust of Coalition troops is based on his questioning of why a Coalition officer would not betray his men, having no tribal or familial obligation to them.

There is nothing wrong with the courage of Muslim fighting men. Given an ideological morale factor, something to believe in, Islam produces the fearful and dreadful mujahedeen, the "Warriors of Allah." It is from this cultural heritage that the suicide bombers and aircraft hijackers have come. Suicide missions have, in the past, been relatively common occurrences. Islam is a faith that mandates holy warriors. That is, warriors whose cause is the defense of the Islamic faith. Islam does not justify suicide, but does permit and reward operations in which there is a high probability that the warrior, in a holy cause, will not survive. This is why the blending of the legal system and the religion is such a powerful and all-embracing belief system.

Commentators on CNN and CNBC constantly

express wonderment that political groups, masquerading as exponents of strict adherence to traditional expressions of Islam, can get suicide bombers, in apparently inexhaustible numbers, to act on this interpretation of the Qur'an. The fact that Muslims are such strong devotees of their faith has more to do with the social structure of the extended family, the deep belief in fatalism and the assumption that life is controlled by an individual's destiny.

Indeed, it is this predestined nature that Islam uses to argue against the individual as an agent of social control. The individual has their own destiny to fulfill, and it is through the individual that Allah's will is implemented. Therefore, the level at which the religious agents and the state operate is through the extended family, and where the community is sufficiently primitive, the tribe.

The foreigner's method of organizing the state and society is of little consequence to someone whose religion is the provider of social justice, social structure and economic arbitration. In the West, foreign affairs are secular, which leaves a gaping hole in the fabric of the society as far as the Muslim can see.

A few years ago there were a number of American and Canadian women in the news who had married Islamic men. After marriage and having one or more children, they had moved to or visited the husband's homeland. The wives were popped into the women's quarters to hang out with their new female in-laws. A divorce or dissertation usually followed and the wives found that their children were automatically in the father's custody under Shari'a. Those women who returned to the West found that they had no legal recourse: Islamic courts would not recognize a

Canadian or American court order addressing custody. The child, by virtue of having an Islamic father, was a citizen of the father's country, and the Shari'a courts refused to recognize the child's claim to American or Canadian citizenship. Most of these matters ended badly with the local Western media accusing their country's legal attachés of failing to provide the mothers with effective consular services.

Much of what the West deems to be important is treated with a fatalistic shrug in Islam. What's to discuss? It's Allah's will and there is nothing that man can do to change that. To even consider trying to thwart Allah's intention is the worst kind of hubris. And hubris is disapproved of very strongly in the Koran.

In contrast, force employed to uphold Islam, which includes the expansion of Islam by military means, is a legitimate use of armed options according to the Koran. In the past, if Muslim armies were successful in war, they were entitled to take booty from the enemy, including slaves. The Koran and Shari'a offer many regulatory admonitions for the conduct of war. For example, there are many examples of Muslim armies approaching battle with non-Muslim forces, when Mohammed and his successor caliphs would offer the non-Muslim side the opportunity to convert to Islam. If the non-Muslim side accepted the offer to embrace Islam, the use of force against them was barred.

If the non-Muslims were "people of the book" (Jews and Christians) and if they rejected the offer to convert, they would be given another offer: they could accept Muslim sovereignty. This meant agreeing to accept Muslim law in their daily activities and agreeing to pay tribute (*jizya*) to the Muslim rulers set over them. Importantly, Jews and Christians could follow their own law privately. The Jews and Christians were the only group to whom the Muslims granted this dispensation. It was granted because they had also received heavenly-revealed scriptures. More importantly, there is a three-paragraph Sunna covering this proper conduct in war. It instructs the faithful that whenever this offer is made to a group qualified to accept the offer and the offer is not accepted, the Muslim armies must fight them. With the sunna clearly enunciated, Muslim armies have engaged in many holy wars. Verse 29 of the Koran is translated for English readers as follows: "Fight the people of the book who do not believe in Allah or the Last Day nor hold as forbidden what has been forbidden by Allah or his apostle [reference to the Prophet of Islam] nor acknowledge the Religion of Truth [Islam] until they pay *Jizya* with willing submission and feel themselves subdued." This is how Islamic expansion largely occurred prior to the fifteenth century.

It was shortly after the migration to Medina that Mohammed received the revelations bearing on the conduct of war against non-Muslims, apostate Muslims and "people of the book." The issue of model conduct in the pursuit of war was added to the Qur'an and Shari'a and given emphasis by an accompanying Sunna.

When we consider the difficulty of going for an Islamic reformation, we must come to terms with the following issues: Islam's prophetic roots, the legal system underpinning the institutional Islamic religion, and the small likelihood of Muslims abandoning these flamboyant incompatibilities, thus permitting grounds for an Islamic balance of retained belief that would allow the West to be seen as something less than an anathema.

For a Muslim country to give anything but lip service to the international rule of law would take a bigger adjustment in the Prophet's revelations than appears likely. To put it more succinctly, there doesn't appear to be a new Treaty of Westphallia in our immediate future. It seems to be pretty obvious that there is currently little perceivable benefit to be gained by the great mass of the Islamic world merging with a globalized rule of law or even partially merging. Certainly, the Islamic media would widely challenge any such merger and make the "streets" aware that such an accommodation would doom Shari'a and therefore Islam.

You might think that surely there are voices to lead a public discussion of such a move to try to make Islam more accommodating to the requirements of the twenty-first century. There are a few leaders, a few intellectuals and a few friends in Western governments, foundations and NGOs who are sympathetic to the destructive path the Islamic world is on, but that's about it.

As to the few intellectuals and governmental officials who would support such a reformation, it is possible to war-game out the probabilities—in spite of the statistical problems related to individual outcomes—that they could all be killed. The power of the fatwa is great and the resources of the street are enormous. The recent murder of Daniel Pearl, the *Wall Street Journal* reporter, reminds us that even if Pakistan's indictments of the killers can be made to stick, we must realize that the life of President Pervez Musharraf of Pakistan is at high risk should someone decide to avenge the killers if they are found guilty. The scary other side of this coin is that the odds that the president of Pakistan will be assassinated change very little, regardless of what happens in the Pearl case.

Chapter Ten

The Outcome as Islamic Civ
Confronts Western Civ

WESTERN CIVILIZATION (AKA Western Civ), the undergraduate course in post-secondary schools, did not prepare us for a world in which civilizations would confront each other on the most fundamental levels. No one who has taken a course in Western Civ for at least the past three generations has been presented with options that extend beyond the Renaissance, the Enlightenment, Thomas Locke, Isaac Newton and democracy as the only way to build an edifying, illuminating and wealth-creating society; a society in which the world continues to unfold in ways that allow us and our progeny to evolve in a safe and expeditious fashion. That's a lot of social conditioning for the elites who govern our media conglomerates, legal system, engineering disciplines and advanced educational management.

The conflict between Western civilization and Islamic civilization is so profound as to defy any solution short of a total reformation by one side or the other, or else an irrevocable, civilization-scale war which humans have never undertaken before.

This conflict can be defined in relatively simple terms that both sides agree upon. Islam is a civilization that is founded on prophetic principles promulgated by the Prophet Mohammed of Mecca. It acknowledges that the rules revealed by the Prophet were given to him by God and as such are not negotiable in any way.

The West is primarily Christian and shares with Islam a borrowed heritage of prophecy via the Judaic part of its cultural heritage. Christianity is a religion of theology that has adapted to a series of crisis-engendered changes in worldview. Its major attribute is that it is geared up to meet fundamental changes in the natural sciences, quantum mathematics and beyond, the social sciences with the requisite encouragement of wide multicultural freedom of thought and freedom of inquiry.

As these two civilizations have evolved, Islam has chosen to view the world as being directed by a master plan, authored by Allah and having characteristics of destiny and fatalism. In contrast to this non-negotiable worldview, the West holds a totally different vision of reality in which the individual is not shackled by a life ordained by predestination in which fatalistic outcomes are unacceptable.

In other words, Islam holds that Allah's plan for the world is immutable and not about to change unless it is His plan to change at this juncture. To the Ulama scholars there is little indication that God has placed a hold on the accuracy of Mohammed's revelations or prophecies. The West regards religion as a matter of individual choice and all rules as secular. Without divine guidance, the Westerner is imbued with a free will that is all-encompassing. The individual is supreme and is inhibited only from acts which will harm others.

Each of these two diametrically opposed views is widely held by the majorities of the populations in the two civilizations, and there are few individuals willing to shift to the other worldview.

It drives Muslim clerics crazy to see the degree to which young Muslims are attracted to Western pop culture and popular iconography, but are young Muslim pop culture fans any different than their elders? These elders are just as prepared to buy technologies from the West without any understanding of how they shape a society.

In Tehran, home of the first successful Islamic revolution and a special religious police force (with a mandate to insure religious conformity), there is a growth industry evidenced by the TV satellite dishes that dot the urban landscape. Through these dishes, Iranians gain access to programs involving nudity, sex, the promotion of alcohol and the advertising of fashion and cosmetics, in spite of rigorous policing of clerically-approved women's apparel and the outlawing of the public use of cosmetics. Paradoxically, all these consumer goods are considered inimical to a devout Muslim life.

More significantly, Tehran is home to a pharmaceutical factory which manufactures, sells, and advertises birth control pills, condoms, diaphragms and other items designed to inhibit contraception, plus nostrums designed and advertised to deal with erectile disfunction, all without interference from the aforementioned religious police.

If this lack of interference by Tehran's religious police—a force hardly having a reputation for being restrained in its responses—seems paradoxical to the reader, it really isn't. Even the most backward Islamic country will willingly buy or produce products of obvious application-level technology. If you want to get on the radar of the religious police, however, try wearing

clothes designed to challenge the authority of the clerical branch of government or doing some basic research
in mathematics or sciences that may alter the prevailing
seventh-century Qur'anic view.

For example, NASA is about to dispatch the first,
and only, Saudi astronaut into space. This faithful son of
Islam wants to know in which direction he should kneel
so he will be facing Mecca when he is up in space. The
answer "any direction" is not one designed to please the
Ulama. Neither are the answers to any questions that,
to achieve a degree of accuracy, require an answer based
on quantum theory. Meanwhile the astronaut is being
castigated from many an imam's pulpit for his heretical
question.

The Ottoman Empire was the last time Islam fielded
a major state. After World War I, Islam was forced to
accept the West's international law. As one of the
defeated powers, the Ottoman Empire had to accept,
along with its concession of defeat, that other
(Western) states were entitled to equal status; thus it
had to grant full recognition of the rights of other
states. At the end of the war the Ottoman Empire
crumbled completely, but some smaller Islamic states
rose and found that the criteria for international recognition was already established and had to be accepted
by all countries. Since all of these post-World War I
Islamic states were on tenuous terms with the international community, they were among the beneficiaries of
the multinational, worldwide desire for stability. The
fragile Islamic states were given stability by their membership in the international community.

After World War II many states that were colonies,
direct or indirect, became inheritors of the decoloniza-
tion process that was encouraged by the United

Nations. They found that the standards of compliance
with statehood were clearly established a priori. At the
same time, there was support in the Islamic states for a
political, legal and social reform movement. The
reformers played on a strong Islamic public sense that
Muslims had been disregarded and Shari'a was not
included in the reference legal systems. The legal scholar reformers, told their constituencies that they would
get the global community to accept the Shari'a as a reference legal system. Islam's lack of centralizing forces
gave the reformers no support at all. Islamist diplomats
who had been learning the hard way the rules by which
international organizations work, said that you didn't
need to be a legal dilettante to get Shari'a accepted in
the big tent. If you wanted to try for that, get a rug merchant from the souk who knew how to negotiate and
bargain.

Abdulla An-Na'im, the Sudanese legal scholar, has an
interesting essay in his book *Toward an Islamic
Reformation*. The essay deals with the Iran–Iraq War and
how it can be explained from the point of view of
Shari'a.

Shari'a is singularly ill-suited to deal with a war
between two Muslim states, according to An-Na'im. It
can offer to mediate, justify and criticize wars between
territorial states, but many Muslims find themselves living in nation-states where the old rules of the territorial state haven't applied since the Treaty of Westphalia.
Shari'a has never had the opportunity to develop
sophisticated legal responses to the nation-state in a
more complex legal environment. At the same time,
governments continue to use the religious power of
Islam to justify actions that are only statecraft.

Shari'a has very little to offer a state operating in a

post-Renaissance environment. It is very strong on medieval problem resolution, but if you have twenty-first century problems like genetic engineering, taxation policies for transnational corporations, the need for legitimating peacekeeping forces to suppress multi-racial, multi-ethnic, multi-language and multi-religious armies, then Shari'a is not the reference legal system you're looking for.

Looking for a way to ensure human rights law that will intrude on someone's age-old custom of having publicly-approbated pogroms, old-fashioned mass murders or gender-related customs like female infanticide or killing a woman because she decided to marry outside of her kinship group or countenances slavery? Once again, Shari'a is not going to offer you much in the way of help. It's called conflict of interest.

Western civilization has moved terribly quickly in the past one hundred years. There are 1.1 billion Muslims wanting to get in on the economic benefits of the West's post-industrial production stream without giving up on the social and cultural benefits of the seventh century.

It's probable that Messrs. Bush and Cheney really believe that the War on Terror is not a war on Islam. It is entirely possible that American Muslims have bought into the American dream. Maybe Bush and Cheney are just a couple of American corporate gunslingers who pulled out their .44's intent only on avenging the heroes of 9/11. If so, the unintended consequence is a war with Islam that not we, nor anyone else, know how to fight.

Chapter Eleven

Are the West and Islam Really Incompatible?

THIS BOOK HAS been dedicated to two friends of the author's, Jackson Matthews and Lily Boyd-Bell, who were in their second year of life when it was written. By the time they have reached young adulthood we will probably have learned how to fight the first intercivilizational war, and they will be of the right age to be soldiers.

What we are talking about here is will our children and grandchildren find themselves in a war of unimagined ferocity, stretching between and within civilizations, because we were unable to find ways to make the two civilizations, Islam and the West, sufficiently compatible?

The War on Terror is really the opening guns of the War Against Islamic Civilization. What the West calls acts of mass terror, the Islamic world calls retribution for the acts of Western governments, of various hues, including wide-ranging aggressions continuing over the past 1,300 years. At the present time, to avoid this war, Islam will have to surrender its extended family and its theocratic state for local administration and a secularization of all its governmental functions.

From the viewpoint of the ordinary Muslim, were Islam to become a collection of secular states, it would be the death of Islam as its adherents understand it. For Muslims, the day-to-day world is focused on the extended family, both socially and economically. This is a limited Muslim world, beset by enemies, whom Islam finds increasingly difficult to hold at bay. Thought of an Islamic reformation is limited to a few intellectuals and layitized lawyers who are without any credibility in the places where it counts—in the mosques, the souks and trading places and with those scholars of Islamic thought, the Ulama.

Islam has a long history that is maintained in an orally-traditioned fashion. This history has had to be transmitted to illiterate people who have learned to navigate camels in various trackless deserts as young boys. Islam has a long history, if not an accurate one, since one of the weaknesses of orally-traditioned history is that it is judged on the grace and the histrionics of the storyteller who recites the history. And don't go giving anyone any lip about spelling history "herstory;" the Muslim world doesn't have a big sense of humour about that sort of thing.

Islamic history begins with the First Crusade (1095–1099), including the sack of Jerusalem by the infidels (unbelievers) with the requisite massacre of the population, pillaging from house to house, rape and looting of the inhabitants. The horrors of the Crusaders and Christians have lightened up many an Arab caravan campfire. The historical verities of Crusader perfidy have been documented in the Islamic tradition as if they were unavenged since yesterday; but in the Islamic world, the Crusades *did* happen only yesterday. Oral histories are bad in their sense of time.

To come to an understanding with Islam would require the West to surrender its open society with all the ramifications that would entail. This would probably please those who defend the concept of allowing police to arrest and hold people without due process of the law as we know it. These are the people who say: "I have nothing to hide. What are you hiding?"

Because of mass communications, the West would have to permit censorship of materials that international organizations agreed not to transmit because they offended the sensibilities of some religion or political regime. Such an agreement would place our open society on the political bargaining table. How long could we hold out when some bargaining chip, like oil or a contribution to a military coalition partnership had become negotiable?

Islam must give up all that is Islam for it to come up with an acceptable negotiating tool. Will the Islamic world willingly abandon the extended family and take on the nuclear family? Will Muslim women give up the security of their role in Islam? It is noteworthy that Pakistan has a woman ambassador to the United States, certainly a good public relations move. But she is questioned by other Pakistani women, and it is said of her that she has no privacy to be with other women. A woman's life in Islam is a parallel life that is a viable other way of organizing a society. Not long ago, most Western women stayed alone at home with children and/or aged parents and longed to get away from the isolated life imposed on them by the nuclear family.

Muslims point out that their world has existed for centuries while the West has been in a constant confusion of roles. While we in the West have become accustomed to generational role/gender shifting, the rest of the world looks on us as hopelessly dysfunctional in our ordinary lifestyles.

One of the things Western immigration data shows is that immigrants from non-Western countries regardless of where they come from—Africa, the Middle East, South-east Asia, South and Central America—regardless of whether their status is legal or illegal, regardless of their preferred destination, have as their primary motivation the achievement of a Western middle-class lifestyle. The only exclusion to this motivation is those immigrants who are genuine political refugees, whose motivation is to avoid being killed or being tortured. This data is very stable for Muslims who immigrate to the West. Muslim immigrants are interested in a middle class life and not interested in abandoning Islam. They are quite faithful in continuing with their gender rules and mosque attendance.

The lesson of the Western reformation is that reformations are so messy, bloody and socially splitting that things must be terribly wrong before anyone in their right mind would choose to be part of a reformation. A reformation is far worse, bloodier and family-dividing than a revolution. The torturing, wars and freelance battles are more than just historical occurrences. The residual bad feelings after a reformation last centuries. Consider the recent reopening of the Muslim-Orthodox wounds of the thirteenth to the fifteenth century's religious wars in the Balkans or the Irish "troubles" which seem to get more and more troubling after the original principals of these wars have gone on with their lives. Reformations have a nasty habit of leaving their religious issues behind to fester and become appropriated as a metaphor for economic, educational and social displacement issues.

Since a reformation is not something anyone wants to take on lightly, and there is no significant enthusiasm apparent in the wider community of Islam for a reformation, the likelihood of a reformation happening is small unless the West encourages it. The 2002 World Cup of Soccer had an interesting sidebar to this issue. The World Cup was played in stadiums in Japan and Korea. In each stadium there was advertising signage around the playing field, and with the exception of one sign, there were no other signs using caligraphy, Arabic script or other non-English alphabetization. All of this in spite of the fact that only spotty American TV rights had been sold, and the total estimated English-speaking TV audience (including the United Kingdom), was only 22 percent of the Russian-speaking TV audience! With English leading the world's commercial languages, to the point of nonexistence of any other languages at an international football game shown on worldwide TV, is it any wonder that people find their culture is held up as insignificant?

Another sidebar comes from a curious little item that appeared through the Reuters wire service about six months before this book was finished. Datelined Shanghai, the item was only about one column inch in length and was buried well inside the newspaper. Its significance, which is quite far-reaching, is belied by its non-descript appearance.

The item reports that the People's Republic Of China, Russia and Tajikistan have signed a formal treaty, known as the Treaty of Shanghai. The report goes on to say that Kazakhstan and other states in the region are expected to sign on immanently. The intent of this treaty is to agree to cooperate in joint military and intelligence-sharing action against Muslim fundamentalist tribal minorities operating in the three countries' territories. Since the publication of this short article there has been little comment about the Treaty of Shanghai's signatories' political moves, but there have been reports of the Chinese People's Liberation Army (PLA) engaging in fairly large battles in tribal enclaves bordering on Singkiang.

Despite what Mr. Putin has said, the Russians have become less than forthcoming about press cooperation in Chechnya while the Russian military has increased its activity there. Meanwhile, in Tajikistan, with its two American bases, things have been abnormally quiet. Taliban refugees have discovered that the country no longer offers the sanctuary available three years ago. Obviously the signatory states of the Treaty of Shanghai have had their ATM PIN codes reactivated and are able to stamp out local "terrorists" to their heart's content.

What is instructive, of course, is that it's not as if this was a new field of operations for any of the participants. The Russian novelist Tolstoy, early in his career as a lieutenant in the Imperial Russian army, wrote a number of short stories from that century's war in Chechnya. Even in 1844, the war had an everlasting quality about it, and the participants had no romantic qualities to endear them.

The skill-sets of the signatories of the Treaty of Shanghai would lead one to expect that we are about to discover just how thin the veneer of civilization really is.

There is one important idea that hasn't been explored here. What if civilizations are subject to evolutionary controls? That is, civilizations are young, they mature and then grow old and die. If this were true, then some manner of civilizations being swept aside would be in the natural order of things.

Notes

1 Francis Throckmorton (1554–1589) was the son of Sir John Throckmorton, who had three Cabinet posts. Francis, an ardent Catholic, was caught plotting a revolt to replace Elizabeth I with Mary Queen of Scots. He was hung, drawn and quartered at Tyburn after Bruno exposed him as a frequent visitor at the French embassy and someone who confessed to Bruno.

2 Rutters in the *quattrocento* were treated as national proprietal charts and maps of harbours showing routes to docks, the locations of dangerous shoals, sandbars, reefs, depth of water, and special information needed to safely enter a harbour. Possession of a rutter by a foreigner was considered evidence of piracy or proof of an attempt or a plot to invade the harbour.

Selected Bibliography

Axworthy, Thomas S. "Doing Evil to Do Good." Paper delivered April 22, 2002. John F. Kennedy School of Government. Harvard University.

An'Naim, Abdulla Ahmed. *Toward an Islamic Reformation: Civil Liberties and International Law*. Syracuse: Syracuse University Press, 1990.

Baigent, Michael and Leigh, Richard. *The Inquisition*. London: Viking-Penguin Books, 1999.

Barber, Benjamine R. *Jihad Vs. McWorld*. New York: Ballantine Books, 1995.

Bergen, Peter L. *Holy War Inc.: Inside the Secret World of Osama bin Laden*. New York: The Free Press, 2001.

Bossy, John *Giordano Bruno and the Embassy Affair*. New Haven and London: Yale University Press, 1991.

Brown, Gillian. *The Consent of the Governed: The Lockean Legacy in Early American Culture*. Cambridge, MA: Harvard University Press, 2001.

Burchard, Johann and Parker, Geoffrey. *At the Court of the Borgias*. London: Folio Society, 1963.

Colidy, Julien, ed. *The Huguenot Wars*. Julie Kernan, trans. Philadelphia: Chilton Book Company, 1969.

Huntington, Samuel P. *The Clash of Civilizations and the Remaking of the New World Order*. New York: Touchstone Books, 1996.

Lewis, Bernard. *The Middle East: 2000 Years of History from the Rise of Christianity till the Present Day*. London: Weidenfield & Nicholson, 1995.

Meyer, Karl E. and Brysak, Shareen Blair. *Tournament of Shadows: The Great Game and Race for Empire in Central Asia*. Washington, D.C.: Counterpoint, 1999.

Milton, Giles. *Nathaniel's Nutmeg: How One Man's Courage Changed the Course of History*. London: Hodder & Stoughton, 1999.

Runciman, Steven. *The First Crusade*. Cambridge: Cambridge University Press, 1951.

Sagan, Carl. *The Demon-Haunted World—Science as a Candle in the Dark*. New York: Ballantine Books, 1997.

Sherman William H. *John Dee: The Politics of Reading and Writing in the English Renaissance*. Amherst, MA: The University of Massachusetts Press, 1995.

Southern, R.W. *The Making of the Middle Ages*. New Haven and London: Yale University Press, 1953.

Index